MEDINA KITCHEN

MEDINA KITCHEN

home cooking from north africa

FIONA DUNLOP

PHOTOGRAPHS BY
SIMON WHEELER

Mitchell Beazley

To Richard – for being there

Medina Kitchen

First published in Great Britain in 2007 by Mitchell Beazley, an imprint of
Octopus Publishing Group Ltd, 2–4 Heron Quays, London E14 4JP

The author and publishers will be grateful for any information that will
assist them in keeping future editions up to date. Although all reasonable
care has been taken in the preparation of this book, neither the publishers
nor the author can accept any liability for any consequence arising from
the use thereof, or the information contained therein.

The author has asserted her moral rights.

ISBN-13: 978-1-84533-265-5
ISBN-10: 1-84533-265-2

A CIP catalogue record for this book is available from the British Library

Set in Helvetica Neue

Colour reproduction by Bright Arts in China

Printed and bound by Toppan Printing Company in China

Commissioning Editor: Rebecca Spry
Editors: Peter Taylor and Leanne Bryan
Executive Art Editor: Nicky Collings
Designers: Simon Wheeler and Fiona Dunlop
Design Assistant: Jonathan Brunton
Photographer: Simon Wheeler
Production Controller: Lucy Carter

CONTENTS

Introduction

Imagine a tiny yellow ball of couscous, like a grain of Saharan sand, rolling across the map from Libya to Tunisia, Algeria and Morocco, then dropping south to Mauritania. These couscous-eating countries define the Maghreb, the 'west' of North Africa. Further east is off the couscous map; further west and you are en route to the Americas. Whatever its exact extent, it paints a picture of a region where a passion for food transcends borders.

At the heart of all Maghrebin cooking lies a deeply rooted sense of hospitality. Bountiful family meals scooped out of a central platter can always accommodate an unexpected guest. Unlike formulaic dishes made to order, this unhurried food is made with love and a deep sense of place. Women rule the kitchen; men do cook, but in the more public realm of restaurants and as banquet organizers, and readily admit that their wives and mothers are behind the most tenderly concocted dishes.

This 'cuisine behind doors' prompted our voyage of gastronomic discovery into private kitchens in Marrakech, Fez, Tunis, Carthage, La Goulette and Tripoli. Each one is unique, and each headed by a personality or two whose character is stamped on the food. Aicha, Latifa, Kenza, Khadouj, Dalila, Mina, Jacob (the only man), and Fozia all cooked what they knew best, revealed a few secrets and shared the stories of their lives. The result is a privileged glimpse into their gastronomic souls.

Food memory

As the exotic fuses with the domestic and jasmine-scented nights slip into mint tea-fuelled days, the people of the medina – the ancient walled town at the heart of a modern city – cook their magic. The beauty of this food is its simplicity. Complex techniques are anathema; the key is specific combinations of ingredients and spices. Yet it is hard to find a more promiscuous cuisine. Subtle games of taste are played as salt and sour mingle with sweet, injected with shards of spice, clouds of fresh herbs, the inebriation of rose, orange-blossom and geranium water, or the soft, sensuous pulp of fruit. Textures are vivid and contrasted, from velvety tagines oozing juices to the layers of delicate, crisp pastry that compose Morocco's masterpiece: pastilla – a pigeon pie combining sweet and savoury flavours that has been lyrically described as 'sweet and peppery, soft and violent'.

A hint of mint, a burst of pomegranate, the tartness of a preserved lemon, the sourness of an olive or the crunch of almonds. The ingredients alone are sensory intoxication. Illiteracy may be high in North Africa, but the food culture soars higher; Maghrebin websites now devote zillions of megabytes to sharing and comparing recipes.

Lay of the land

The huge geographical variations across the Maghreb start from Libya's deep south, the Fezzan, where Colonel Gaddafi's policy of 'desert greening' brings unexpected vegetables to the rippling sand dunes of the Sahara. Then, in arid southern Morocco, there is the argan tree: from the kernel of the fruit comes a strong, nut-flavoured oil, increasingly sought after in the West for its high vitamin E content. In the milder north, secluded valleys harbour cherry orchards, while orange groves, fruit orchards and vineyards blanket the flatter terrain. In Libya, the coastal strip is chequered with wheat, barley and peanut fields and, like all of the northern Maghreb, silvery olive groves. On scrubby hillsides everywhere, long-eared sheep nibble at wild herbs, ensuring ultra-succulent lamb. Then there is thick, unrefined honey, from wild oregano, orange blossom, or cedar forests, trailing a path of nectar across the hills of North Africa.

From outside in: culinary crosscurrents

Despite sharing the Pillars of Islam and couscous, these three countries have experienced quite different culinary cross-fertilization. They all, however, started with the indigenous Berbers, who developed couscous (*seksu* in Berber), allegedly in the mountains of Algeria, between the 11th and 13th centuries. In North Africa, couscous takes centre stage every Friday, the Muslim sabbath. Then come the contents of the spice cupboard, richly coloured, pungent, medicinal, exotic. One of the first known food imports, garlic, travelled from Central Asia via ancient Egypt. Along the same route came cinnamon, believed by the Romans to possess sacred qualities and burned in industrial quantities by Emperor Nero at his mother's funeral. At the same time came caravan-loads of coriander, cardamom, saffron, cumin, turmeric and sesame seeds. North African alchemy subsequently conjured up mixes such as Tunisia's *tabel* (coriander, caraway, garlic and red chilli pepper), *bharat* (cinnamon, black pepper and dried rosebuds) and Morocco's *ras-el-hanout* (composed of 15–30 spices).

Phoenicians, Greeks, Romans and Carthaginians all planted the seeds of their gastro-obsessions, whether olives, citrus fruits (the lemon came later, around the 10th century) or grapevines. All have endured, including wine production. In the 7th century, together with Islam, Arab invaders brought Middle Eastern foods, farming techniques and the fine culinary arts of Persia. Fastforward 900 years and this pot of exotica was further refined by the Moors and Jews expelled from Spain. Their Andalucian input, which included the chickpea and pastilla, reigns supreme in the northern Moroccan towns of Meknes, Rabat, Tetouan and, above all, Fez. In contrast, Marrakech's early influences were more Berber mixed with West African.

In Libya, Algeria and Tunisia, around 300 years of the Ottoman Empire have etched themselves deep on the palate. Stuffed vegetables (*dolma*) and almond-filled pastries come straight from the Bosphorus, while *warka* (gossamer-thin pastry) is thought to have come from China via Persia. Once the Ottoman sun had set, Tunisia and Libya respectively underwent French and Italian colonization, bringing obvious legacies such as pasta, ricotta and tomato paste. Put all the above next to 400 varieties of Saharan dates and other indigenous delicacies, and it becomes clear that Maghrebin cuisine is, in the apt words of a Moroccan king, 'rooted in Africa, watered by Islam and rustled by the winds of Europe'.

Morocco: tagines and sauces

The forte of Moroccan cooks are tagines, developed in many variations and named after the funnel-shaped terracotta dish in which the food is slow-cooked. Its hallmark is a reduced sauce of complex flavours. Many tagines integrate the sweetness of dried fruit. Some form of sweet flavour – from icing sugar to cinnamon, honey or fruit – is added to most recipes. Sixty or so combinations of meat or fish and vegetables can be cooked in one of four sauces, with specific vegetables affecting the flavour of each meat. The first, *m'qualli*, is a yellow sauce made from oil, ginger, onion, saffron, salt and occasionally a bunch of coriander; *m'hammer*, a red sauce, is composed of butter, sweet paprika, garlic, saffron, ginger and onion; *k'dra*, a lighter, yellow sauce, contains onions, butter, pepper, salt and saffron; finally *m'charmel*, a red sauce, combines sweet paprika, garlic, cumin and coriander.

Tunisia: land of harissa

The world has been lured by Tunisia's balmy climate, fertile soil and inspirational produce. Tiny in comparison with Morocco or Libya but with a far more modern society, its rich cuisine goes well beyond the *brik à l'oeuf* of tourist restaurants. It is the hottest of the three cuisines due to a love of harissa, that fiery chilli pepper paste. Middle-class Tunisians cannot decide whether they are Tunisian or French, hence their food has a strong Gallic accent. With this European perspective, Tunisians look down on Libyans as country bumpkins and know surprisingly little about Moroccan cooking.

Tunisian bourgeois food culture has its own rules; for example, the only salads considered authentic are *méchouia* (grilled peppers with onions, tomato and garlic) and carrot and potato salads; anything else is 'imported'. Lamb and chicken should never be eaten with tomatoes but with cinnamon or saffron and *smen* (clarified butter), while the combination of sweet and savoury (such as meat and fruit) is only for special occasions. Whereas 'tagine' is a slow-cooked stew to Moroccans, for Tunisians, stew is *ragout* or *marquit*, and a tagine is more like a baked Spanish tortilla or Moroccan pastilla.

Libya: soup specialists

Libya produced antiquity's wonderfood, *silphium*. This resin from a giant fennel, now extinct, was used as a rich seasoning and was considered a contraceptive. Modern Libyan food is less recherché, more simple and punchy. The once nomadic Tuaregs of the Sahara are known for desert fare such as flatbread baked in the sand eaten with *burgam*, a green paste of flour, oil, water and herbs. Their bittersweet tea is a brew so potent that it is nicknamed 'tea espresso'. Another rural basic is *bazin*, a paste of barley, salt and water. Things look up along the coastal belt, not least in healthy breakfasts of fresh white cheese, plump tomatoes, juicy dates and black olives.

Although the Libyan approach to food is light years from the subtleties of neighbouring Tunisia, they excel in two areas: soups and desserts. Patisserie shops produce divine concoctions inherited from the Italians as well as Ottoman-style pastries or more restrained date, semolina and pistachio cakes. Everything, everywhere is washed down with mint tea.

Kitchen flux

Following on from this multi-layered past, 21st-century North African cooking is changing again. Short cuts such as pressure cookers, blenders and vacuum-packed *warka* have followed the oven, introduced relatively recently, but there is now an increasing awareness of diet and nutrition. Moroccan kitchens are being galvanized by Choumicha, a young TV chef whose daily programmes and food magazine promote a kind of 'Moroccan-lite' cuisine. Tunisia, with better education, stronger links to France and an indelible passion for *poisson*, has a naturally healthy, balanced diet, while in Libya the cuisine is the least hallowed and therefore most open to change.

One contemporary influence hard to ignore in Morocco is that of expatriate Westerners who, although shadowing the rock 'n' roll writers and artists of the 1960s, are less interested in blowing their minds, and more in seducing their palates. Thus a new generation of incomers are goading the *tadelakt*-walled designer palaces of Marrakech into ever more gastronomic innovation. Luckily for the rest of us, the untouchables remain.

Bil hana wal shefa! (or 'Happy eating!')

MARRAKECH

Aicha Ait Ouad

'HER SHYNESS OCCASIONALLY DISSOLVES INTO GIGGLES, YET HER MEASURED, CALM APPROACH WORKS WONDERS WITH THE FOOD.'

Like a princess in an exquisite treasure box, Aicha cooks for us in the very heart of Marrakech at the 15th-century Ksour Agafay, one of the city's first grand residences and now a private members' club and occasional cultural venue. This is where Aicha often works for Kenza Melehi and Abel Damoussi, the dynamic couple who own the Ksour and who are permanently on the go between their cultural and business interests. When the Damoussis switch residence in the Marrakech region or go north to Kenza's family on the Atlantic coast, she follows uncomplainingly. 'It's only when they're abroad that I finally relax!' she jokes.

In her late 30s, Aicha looks youthful and poised, and it is hard to imagine her toiling away among the pots and pans of her employers. Her shyness occasionally dissolves into giggles, yet her measured, calm approach works wonders with the food. She is able to knock together several main courses, starters and a dessert in a few hours without even a bead of perspiration – and Marrakech, desert city that it is, can be hot. In contrast, her dishes are relatively light, leaning towards the more digestible, healthier methods preached by Morocco's TV chef Choumicha. These are also what her employers require, as Kenza, a fashion designer, is slim and wants to stay that way.

'I love working alone with Madame Kenza as I learn so much,' says Aicha. 'At home I picked up a lot from my mother, who did all the cooking, but my father also used to cook for big weddings and banquets. That means I'm used to food being prepared on a large scale. Sometimes Monsieur and Madame entertain dozens of people and I have to be able to manage that.' She smiles in her wonderfully serene way: 'It's not a problem.'

Aicha's round, open face and honey colouring is typical of the Berbers, the original inhabitants of Morocco, so it is not surprising to learn that her native home is Asni, a small town on the slopes of the High Atlas Mountains south of Marrakech. When the Arabs marched into Morocco in the 7th century, the mountains became the Berbers' territory. Most of Aicha's family (three sisters, one brother and a few half siblings) still live in Asni and she herself worked there as a weaver until five years ago. That led to another of her talents that she enjoys during her spare time. 'I love sewing, doing embroidery and making kaftans,' she explains, revealing a creative bent which reappears in her food. 'What I love most in Asni is that everything is cooked on coals or on a wood fire. It tastes ten times better. Couscous cooked on a wood fire is really something else.' This is genuine, discerning gastro-passion. 'They also have lots of different kinds of breads. And after eating dinner there I fall asleep very easily!' Despite her talent for 'light' cuisine, at heart Aicha remains a mountain girl with a big appetite.

'My favourite place to work is the Kasbah,' she continues, referring to a rambling castle just outside Marrakech, and now an exclusive hotel owned by the Damoussis. 'The gardens there give me loads of fresh ingredients. They grow thyme, coriander, mint and masses of vegetables, such as tomatoes, carrots, aubergines, cauliflower and mini courgettes – all delicious and fresh.' The Kasbah grounds are vast, lush and prolific, despite the sandy horizon punctuated by date palms and the occasional passing camel. 'I also enjoy working here in the medina, as it's so beautiful,' she says. 'The neighbourhood is wonderful for shopping. I buy all the vegetables in the street markets, above all on Fridays when people come from outside Marrakech to sell homegrown produce. For fish and meat I go to Guéliz (the new town of Marrakech) as you get a better quality there and you can be sure it's fresh. As for herbs and spices, if I can, I buy them from people who come down from the mountains as those are the best and freshest.' Clearly Aicha's rural childhood has given her an instinctive feel for the finest ingredients, the hallmark of her cuisine.

On her nights off, when not visiting relatives, she joins the smoke, drums, story tellers, dancing snakes and frenetic atmosphere of Djema El F'naa, the vast square which constitutes the heart of the old city. 'I go to stall number 31,' she beams, referring to one of the dozens of outdoor kitchens. 'They make very good food. My favourite is couscous with sheep's head. The other dish I love in Marrakech is *tanjia Marrakchia*. That's a mutton stew traditionally made by men and cooked for hours in the ashes of the ovens where they heat water for the *hammams* (steam baths). The ingredients are really simple – just mutton, garlic and spices – but the length of slow-cooking and ashes give it an exceptional flavour and texture.'

Although her tastes are rooted in tradition, Aicha admits to being hooked on Choumicha, Morocco's homegrown version of Nigella Lawson. In a gastronomic flash, this innovative young chef has conquered the home cooks of Morocco and, not least, given Aicha plenty of ideas. 'I have a TV in the kitchen and watch her daily at midday,' she confessess. 'Choumicha does regional Moroccan food. She even went to Asni! She also makes a few international dishes. Unfortunately I can't cook many of them – just steak and a few soups – but I love eating international food when I can. I've never travelled outside Morocco but I've been to Fez, Asilah, Casablanca, Rabat, Tiznit and Essaouira. The place I love most though is Imlil, up in the Atlas Mountains near where I was born. It's very beautiful and there are lots of fruit – peaches, apples, apricots, pears, plums, walnuts...' She pauses for a minute. 'Walnuts are wonderful in lamb tagine with figs!' It's that mountain girl speaking again.

MARRAKECH: OASIS OF PLENTY

Fragrant hedges of rosemary and fig trees surround one of Marrakech's most exquisite monuments, the Saadian Tombs, a masterpiece of intricate mosaic patterns, delicate plasterwork and thin marble columns. This is where the sultans of Marrakech have slumbered for 500 years, while above them the ripened figs plummet to the ground and rosemary perfumes the air. Yet, only a few steps away, the labyrinthine medina heaves with commercial chaos between specialist souks, informal street markets and the performances and budget food stalls of Djema El F'naa. Here, motorbikes buzz through the backstreets, weaving between shoppers who might be Western glamour pusses, gawping tourists, local lads in baseball hats or women in long, hooded *djellabas* revealing just a flash of henna-tattooed ankle. Marrakech, more than anywhere else in North Africa, is a city on the cusp.

In the background loom the pinky mud-brick walls that surround this hot and dusty 1,000-year-old oasis town – the most African, the most frenetic, and the most cosmopolitan of Morocco's cities. Bohemian too, as, back in the 1960s, Yves Saint-Laurent, Mick Jagger, William Burroughs and John Paul Getty Jr were just a few of the celebs and idle rich kids seduced by the cobalt skies and the lofty palm trees silhouetted against the snowcapped Atlas Mountains. One of the city's new residents was the American chef Robert Carrier, one of the first to seriously investigate what was then a little-known cuisine. Today, many chefs at the upmarket restaurants and riads (traditional houses with an interior garden) hail from abroad, and their elevated cooking pulls out all the stops.

What changes little is daily life, with gloriously fresh food at every turn, though never on as large a scale as at the gargantuan Marché Central of Tunis. What Marrakech has, instead, are neighbourhood markets that set up every morning on the shady side of the street, as well as occasional specialized ones such as the egg market, where skyscrapers of egg trays obscure their sellers. At their feet, squawking caged chickens await their fate. There are preserved lemons, plump violet olives, fat dates from the south, piles of freshly baked flatbreads and sacks of couscous grain, chickpeas and lentils.

Dotted among the labyrinthine byways of the souk are the shifty purveyors of herbs and spices. The coloured powders and suspended bunches of herbs are attributed extraordinary medicinal properties by their vendors; a scant few are destined purely for cookery. The legendary *ras-el-hanout* (see page 187) comes in various forms and the most expensive ingredient is always saffron. Over 150,000 crocus flowers are needed to make just one kilo. The fine, intensely fragrant strands (the red stigmas of *Crocus sativus*), command wildly varying prices according to quality and the client. It remains the spice par excellence, which first travelled from its Kashmiri source to Morocco over 1,000 years ago.

Into an alleyway comes a donkey led by a wizened, wide-hatted Berber keeping an eagle eye on the paniers overflowing with silvery sardines. Behind him is a cart piled high with sunshine-yellow honeydew melons, juicy figs, glossy purple plums and velvet-skinned peaches. Later, as the setting sun paints the sky behind the great Koutoubia Minaret, shadows cloak the flaking pink walls and mysterious cul-de-sacs. Skinny cats slip around corners, boys kick footballs, housewives bring their dough to the neighbourhood oven, and another rooftop cocktail party kicks in. Medieval meets 21st century and North meets South: Marrakech has become a mesmerizing cultural hybrid.

Soupe à la citrouille   Pumpkin soup

This simple, healthy, autumnal soup puts pumpkin centre stage and enhances the subtle flavour with a gentle kick of harissa. Use chopped basil instead of parsley, if you wish.

serves 4

500g (1lb 2oz) pumpkin, peeled, deseeded and cut into large chunks
500ml (18fl oz) chicken or vegetable stock
50g (1¾oz) cooked chickpeas
½ tsp ground black pepper
½ tsp harissa (see page 186), or to taste
leaves from a bunch of flat leaf parsley, finely chopped
salt, to taste
1 tbsp extra-virgin olive oil

1 - Put the pumpkin in a saucepan with the stock and simmer gently for 10–15 minutes. Allow to cool, transfer to a blender with the cooking water and whiz to a smooth consistency.

2 - Return the mixture to a saucepan, stir in the chickpeas, pepper, harissa and parsley and heat through. Season with salt. Drizzle each bowl with a thread of olive oil before serving.

Bessara   Broad bean and garlic soup

Broad beans are being rediscovered for their high protein and folic acid content, but have been around for 5,000 years, since the ancient Egyptians. The Berber name for this Moroccan classic is *talsha*; in Arabic it is *bessara*. Whatever the label, Aicha's health-conscious employer, Kenza, is an enthusiast.

serves 4

1 litre (1¾ pints) water
500g (1lb 2oz) fresh broad beans, shelled and skinned, or 250g (9oz) dried broad beans, soaked overnight, drained and rinsed
4 garlic cloves, peeled and crushed
salt, to taste
3–4 tbsp extra-virgin olive oil, plus extra to drizzle
1 tsp paprika
1 tsp ground cumin (see page 186)
squeeze of lemon juice

1 - Bring the water to the boil in a saucepan, then add the broad beans, garlic and salt. Reduce the heat and simmer for 30 minutes. If using dried broad beans, triple the cooking time.

2 - Transfer to a blender and whiz with the olive oil and spices. Adjust the salt, if necessary.

3 - Serve with a drizzle of olive oil and a light squeeze of lemon juice.

Zaalouk aux tomates
Mashed aubergine, tomato and garlic salad

Grating tomatoes is a classic Moroccan technique. An excellent *passata di pomodoro* can be produced when really juicy tomatoes are used. *Zaalouk* is traditionally a purée made with fried aubergines, but Aicha's steamed version is kinder on the figure and leaves the aubergines in an informally mashed, silken state. There are endless modifications: the aubergines can be replaced with courgettes, or you could use half and half. *Zaalouk* is eaten warm or chilled and becomes more intensely flavoured if allowed to stand for an hour or so.

serves 4–6

3 aubergines
sea salt, to taste
3–4 plump, juicy tomatoes
4–6 garlic cloves, peeled and crushed
leaves from a bunch of coriander, finely chopped
2 tsp ground cumin (see page 186)
1 tsp ground white pepper
2 tsp sweet paprika
squeeze of lemon juice
extra-virgin olive oil, to drizzle

1 - Half-peel the aubergines to leave vertical stripes of skin, wash, then chop into chunks. Sprinkle with sea salt and leave to drain in a colander for 30 minutes to allow the juices to seep out. Rinse and pat dry with paper towels.

2 - Put the aubergine in a steamer, steam for 15 minutes then return to the colander. Steam in batches if necessary. Break it up roughly with the back of a spoon to create a semi-mash and to get rid of any liquid. Set aside.

3 - Cut the tomatoes in half and grate into a pan, discarding the skin. Add the garlic, half the coriander, the cumin, pepper and paprika, then cook over a low heat for about 20 minutes until you have a thick sauce.

4 - Stir the aubergines into the sauce and sprinkle with the remaining coriander. Just before serving, squeeze over lemon juice, to taste, and drizzle with olive oil.

Salade de fèves   Broad bean salad

Ibawen, the name of this dish in Aicha's native language, Berber, is a delicious and filling summer starter. It is straightforward to prepare once you have accomplished the laborious shelling and skinning. It is only worth making with fresh broad beans, so find a kitchen helper if necessary!

serves 4–6

bunch of flat leaf parsley
1kg (2lb 4oz) fresh broad beans, shelled and skinned
1 tsp salt, or to taste
1–2 tsp ground cumin (see page 186)
1–2 tsp sweet paprika
3 tbsp extra-virgin olive oil
3 garlic cloves, peeled and crushed
2–3 small dried chilli peppers
leaves from a bunch of coriander, finely chopped
leaves from a bunch of flat leaf parsley, finely chopped
juice of 1 lemon
1 preserved lemon (see page 187), finely sliced, to garnish

1 - Put half the bunch of parsley in the bottom of a steamer and place the beans on top. Lightly salt the beans. Put the other half of the bunch of parsley on top. Steam for about 15 minutes.

2 - Mix the spices together in a bowl with the olive oil, garlic and chilli peppers and cook in a saucepan over a medium heat for a couple of minutes.

3 - Add the beans (but not the parsley cooked with them), coriander, chopped parsley and lemon juice, and turn over in the warm dressing to coat evenly. Serve warm or cold, garnished with slices of preserved lemon.

Salade de tomates caramelisées   Caramelized tomato salad

This pretty and unusual starter is a toned-down version of the very sweet Fassi tomato confit.
It is quicker to prepare and easier to eat in quantity. Eat with two or three other salads and some
flatbread (see page 44).

serves 6

> **2kg (4lb 8oz) plump, juicy tomatoes**
> **1 tbsp olive oil**
> **1 tsp ground cinnamon**
> **2–3 tbsp granulated sugar**
> **salt, to taste**
> **handful of sesame seeds, to garnish**

1 - Make a cross at the base of each tomato and plunge them into boiling water for 30 seconds.
  Transfer to cold water. Drain and remove the loosened skins. Cut in half and remove the seeds.
2 - Put the olive oil, cinnamon and sugar in large pan, mix, then add the tomatoes. Cook for 15–20
  minutes over a low heat, stirring continuously until the mixture is reduced and caramelized.
3 - Arrange in a serving dish, season with salt and garnish with sesame seeds.

M'kouar   Cabbage and raisin salad

This salty-sweet combination works surprisingly well. It is also a perfect accompaniment to roast
pork. Alternatively, serve with foie gras as an unusual and elegant starter.

serves 4

> **knob of butter**
> **1 tbsp olive oil**
> **1kg (2lb 4oz) white cabbage, shredded**
> **1 tsp ground ginger**
> **150g (5½oz) raisins**

1 - Heat the butter and olive oil in a frying pan, then add the cabbage. Stir quickly over a medium
  heat then reduce the heat and cover the pan for about 10 minutes to steam the cabbage.
2 - When the cabbage is soft, add the ginger and raisins, stirring well. Simmer gently over a low
  heat with the lid off and stirring occasionally, for a further 15 minutes or until the mixture has
  caramelized slightly.

Salade d'épinards aux olives et citrons confits
Spinach, olive and preserved lemon salad

The first references to spinach are from Sasanian Persia (about AD 226–640) and when it reached China it became known as the 'Persian green'. The first mention of it in the Mediterranean was in the 10th-century medical work of Al-Razi and in two agricultural treatises, one by Ibn Wahshiya, the other by Qustus al-Rumi. With that knowledge under your belt, this salad should be doubly satisfying.

serves 4–6

2kg (4lb 8oz) spinach, roughly chopped
knob of butter
1 tbsp olive oil
2–3 garlic cloves, peeled and crushed
1 tsp ground black pepper
salt, to taste
1 tsp ground cumin (see page 186)
juice of ½ lemon

to garnish:
leaves from 3–4 stems of flat leaf parsley, finely chopped
handful of pitted black olives
1 preserved lemon (see page 187), finely sliced
extra-virgin olive oil, to drizzle

1 - Steam the spinach for about 5 minutes.

2 - In a large pan heat the butter, olive oil, the garlic, pepper, salt and cumin. Add the spinach and sauté for about 5 minutes. Add the lemon juice and remove from the heat.

3 - Garnish with the chopped parsley, black olives, slices of preserved lemon and a generous drizzle of olive oil.

Tajine de poisson au safran, échalotes et raisins
Saffron fish tagine with shallots and sultanas

This dish is a great way of preparing robust, white, low-cost fish that you might not otherwise eat, but be careful not to overcook it. The balance of saffron and sultanas with the slippery shallots works very well. Aicha has a clever trick of peeling the onion and shallots in a bowl of water to avoid weeping inconsolably into the tagine.

serves 4

1 cinnamon stick, roughly broken
1 large onion, peeled and finely sliced into rounds
2 tbsp olive oil
1 tsp ground ginger
1 tsp ground black pepper
1 tsp saffron, plus 4–5 extra pinches
1 tsp sweet paprika
1kg (2lb 4oz) robust white fish fillet (such as pollock) skinned, boned and cut into
   large chunks
500g (1lb 2oz) whole shallots, peeled
125g (4½oz) sultanas, soaked in water for 20 minutes
250ml (9fl oz) water

1 - Sprinkle the cinnamon over the bottom of a tagine dish or a large, wide pan, then lay the onion rounds on top.

2 - In a bowl, mix together the olive oil, ginger, pepper, 1 tsp saffron and paprika. Add the chunks of fish and marinate for a minimum of 10 minutes.

3 - Meanwhile, steam the shallots for about 15 minutes, to part-cook them.

4 - Lay the fish pieces on top of the onion rings, leaving some of the marinade behind, and place the shallots on top to cover. If you like a spicy dish, increase the amount of marinade sauce by adding more oil and spices. Stir the extra pinches of saffron into the marinade and spoon over the fish–shallot mixture. Sprinkle with the soaked sultanas and pour the water around the edge of the dish or pan.

5 - Cover the dish or pan and cook over a medium heat for about 15 minutes, or until cooked through. Remove the fish with a slotted spoon and keep warm, then cook the sauce for a further 10 minutes, lid removed, to reduce. Serve in a wide dish to show off the ingredients.

Tajine d'agneau aux figues et abricots
Lamb tagine with figs and apricots

This is more melt-in-the-mouth stuff out of the Moroccan kitchen, a classic marriage between fruit and meat, not too sweet and not at all complicated to prepare. It will disappear instantly as soon as it hits the table. As a grand finale, you can scatter the dish with walnut kernels to give it a touch of Aicha's mountain-village style.

serves 4–6

1kg (2lb 4oz) boned shoulder of lamb, cut into large chunks
1 large onion, peeled and diced
1 cinnamon stick, roughly broken
2–3 tsp ground black pepper
3 tsp ground ginger
1 tsp saffron
1 tsp ground cinnamon
1 tsp sweet paprika
1 tbsp olive oil
2 tbsp vegetable oil

fruit mixture:
250g (9oz) dried figs
150g (5½oz) dried pitted apricots
1 tsp ground cinnamon
1 tbsp caster sugar
3 tsp orange-blossom water
about 175–250ml (6–9fl oz) water

1 - Put all the meat dish ingredients into a wide, deep pan over a medium heat, stir briefly then almost cover with water. Cover with a lid, then simmer gently for 1–1½ hours. Check the moisture level occasionally, adding more water if necessary.

2 - Meanwhile, make the fruit mixture. Steam the figs and apricots for about 15 minutes until soft and moist. Put them in a saucepan and add the rest of the fruit mixture ingredients. Simmer over a low heat for about 30 minutes. If the mixture gets too dry, add some cooking juice from the meat to moisten.

3 - When the meat is cooked through, remove the lid and, without removing the meat, simmer for about 10 minutes to reduce the sauce. Transfer the meat to a serving dish, spoon over the reduced sauce, then arrange the fruit mixture around it.

Djaje belimoune   Chicken with orange and saffron

This dish, invented by Aicha herself, is guaranteed to provide another intense, ambrosial experience. The strong saffron flavour blends brilliantly with the chicken while the fresh-tasting, tender orange pieces add another dimension. The pulp tears away easily from the rind while eating. It would look spectacular as the main course for a dinner party.

serves 6

6 chicken pieces
1 cinnamon stick
1 tsp ground black pepper
1 tsp ground ginger
4–5 pinches of saffron
1 tsp yellow-orange colouring, or turmeric (optional)
1 tsp salt
1 tbsp olive oil
2 tbsp vegetable oil
250ml (9fl oz) orange juice

orange mixture:
2 large, unwaxed oranges
juice of 1 orange
1 cinnamon stick, roughly broken
1 tsp ground cinnamon
2½ tbsp caster sugar
handful of sesame seeds (optional), to garnish

1 - Put the chicken pieces in a large deep saucepan with the spices, colouring, salt and oils. Stir to combine, then simmer over a low heat for about 10 minutes. Add most of the orange juice, cover the pan and simmer vigorously for about 20 minutes. Turn the chicken pieces over about halfway through the cooking time. Add the remaining orange juice, reduce the heat and simmer gently for a further 20 minutes, or until the chicken is cooked through.

2 - Meanwhile, prepare the orange mixture. Cut the oranges into segments, remove any pith or seeds but keep the skin on. Place them in a saucepan with the orange juice, a few spoonfuls of water, the two kinds of cinnamon and the sugar. Reduce over a medium heat for about 20–30 minutes, or until no juice is left and the mixture has caramelized.

3 - Lift the chicken pieces out of the pan with a slotted spoon and place on a wide serving dish. Pour over the sauce from the pan and spoon over the orange mixture. Garnish with a sprinkling of sesame seeds.

Tajine d'agneau aux tomates et boules d'amandes
Lamb tagine with tomato and almond balls

Although testing to prepare, the end result of this tagine makes it well worth the effort. It is one of Aicha's more unusual recipes; she confesses to getting bored with the straightforward ones.

serves 6

large knob of butter
2 tbsp olive oil
1½kg (3lb 5oz) boned shoulder of lamb, cut into large chunks
2 large onions, peeled and finely chopped
pinch of saffron
1 tsp ground ginger, or finely chopped fresh ginger
½ tsp ground white pepper
1 tsp each *ras-el-hanout* (see page 187) and turmeric
2 cinnamon sticks
1 bay leaf
bunch of flat leaf parsley, tied
about 500ml (18fl oz) water
2kg (4lb 8oz) tomatoes
1 tsp ground cinnamon
dash of olive oil, plus extra for sautéing the almonds
1 heaped tbsp granulated sugar
500g (1lb 2oz) blanched almonds, plus 12–15 extra
100g (3½oz) sesame seeds

1 - Heat the butter and olive oil in a large saucepan and cook the lamb over a medium heat until it is lightly browned. Add the onion, spices (apart from the ground cinnamon), bay leaf, parsley and the water to cover. Cover the pan with a lid and simmer over a low heat for 1 hour, stirring occasionally, until the lamb is cooked through. Check the mixture occasionally and add a little more water if it gets too dry.

2 - In the meantime, skin the tomatoes. Make a cross at the base of each tomato and plunge them into boiling water for 30 seconds. Transfer to cold water. Drain and remove the loosened skins. Chop and put in a separate pan. Add the ground cinnamon, olive oil and sugar. Cover and simmer gently for 1 hour, stirring occasionally.

3 - Preheat the oven to 110°C/225°F/Gas mark ¼. Heat a little olive oil in a frying pan over a medium heat and sauté the 500g (1lb 2oz) almonds until lightly browned. Put about half the quantity in a blender and grind coarsely, then stir into the tomato mixture to create a paste.

4 - In a bowl, form the tomato paste into balls, then roll them in the sesame seeds and poke a whole almond into each ball. Keep these warm in the preheated oven until ready to eat.

5 - Serve the lamb in a wide dish, pour over the sauce, then decorate with the almond balls.

Tarte aux figues
Fig cake

You need to find really juicy figs to do justice to this autumnal cake. It is light, moist and looks deceptively unassuming.

serves 6–8

3 large eggs, beaten

3½ tbsp caster sugar

3 tbsp vegetable oil, plus extra for oiling the dish

2 tbsp plain yogurt

finely grated zest of 1 unwaxed orange

4 heaped tbsp plain flour, plus extra for sprinkling

14g (½oz) easy-blend dried yeast

7g (¼oz) vanilla powder (one small packet), or 1 tsp vanilla extract

16 fresh, juicy figs, cut into quarters or sixths

orange glaze:

juice of 3 oranges

1–2 tbsp caster sugar

1 - Preheat the oven to 180°C/350°F/Gas mark 4. In a large bowl, whisk together the eggs, sugar, oil, yogurt, orange zest and flour. Add the yeast and vanilla and whisk to a smooth, elastic consistency.

2 - Oil a wide tart or quiche dish with a removable bottom and sprinkle with flour. Pour in the mixture, then lay the figs on top in a regular pattern, seed-side upwards (they will inevitably sink). Bake in the preheated oven for 20–30 minutes, or until the crust is a deep golden brown.

3 - To make the orange glaze, cook the orange juice and sugar in a saucepan over a low heat and simmer until thickened.

4 - When the cake is baked, allow to cool a little, then transfer to a flat plate. Allow to cool completely, then pour over the orange glaze.

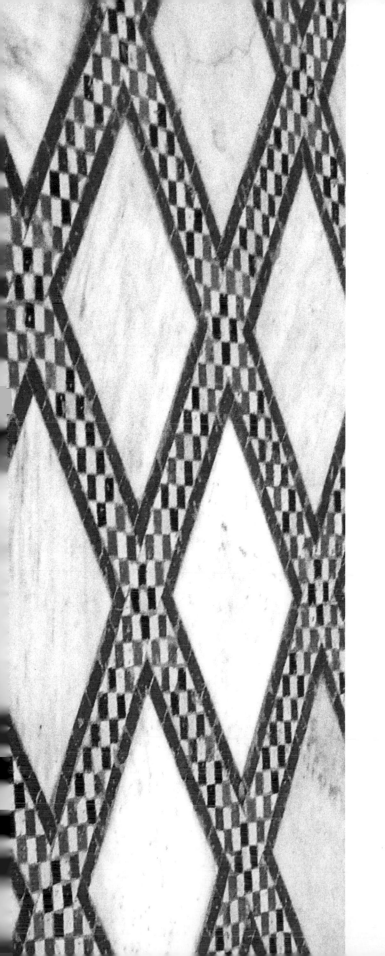

FEZ

فارس

Latifa Alaoui  لطيفة

'WITH TAGINES, YOU NEED TO FIND A VEGETABLE THAT SUITS THE TYPE OF MEAT AND THEN THE SPICES THAT SUIT BOTH. EVEN THE WAY YOU CUT AN ONION IS IMPORTANT.'

Latifa Alaoui is a strong, intelligent and discreet women who has developed numerous facets having been a working mother from early on in her life. Cooking is high on her list of talents, and even more so now she has the leisure time to indulge in it, surrounded by her extended family. This includes Laila, a vivacious 33-year-old law graduate who recently married Anas, the youngest of Latifa's three sons. Between the two of them, they can cook virtually anything from the Fassi (Fassi meaning 'from Fez') epicurean repertoire, although it is Latifa, with her long years of experience, who creates delicate little pastries, ultra-refined pastilla or a sumptuous couscous. In their combined cooking sessions there emerges such affection, complicity and humour that they are an exemplary duo of mother and daughter-in-law. All the clichés fly out the window.

Born and bred into the great Alaoui family of Fez, Latifa left home when she married at the tender age of 13, and lived for years in Rabat and Meknes before settling in the seaside town of El Jdida, a former Portuguese port just south of Casablanca. Yet the pull of her native city is magnetic, and Latifa often returns to stay in her brother's holiday home, a delightful corner house that is the Fez mini equivalent of New York's Flatiron Building. Childhood friends live round the corner and the sprawling Rcif market is just a few minutes' walk away. Off the house's triangular patio, with its dizzy blue and white tiling, is a small but functional kitchen where a four-burner gas cooker acts as the stage for Latifa and Laila's elaborate concoctions. Across the patio is a traditional Moroccan salon lined with low couches and cushions where, like most of female Morocco, they tune in to watch TV chef Choumicha and her modern take on traditional food. It also makes a cool retreat for a post-prandial siesta, with easily enough room for half a dozen guests to stretch out and daydream.

'It saddens me to see Fez being abandoned,' says Latifa. 'So many Fassis have left for Casablanca or Rabat. But then other friends are setting up small hotels and staying on. It's certainly changing.' She gives a sizzling pan a vigorous stir. 'I actually had my three sons here in Fez in the early 1960s, the first when I was only 15. But as my husband was a teacher, we lived all over Morocco. We also travelled abroad a lot, to France, of course, to London and to different parts of Spain, always by car so as not to miss anything. I love the experience of new landscapes and I've also discovered lots on the cooking front. I've sampled Turkish and Lebanese cuisine, and Algerian too. It's very different from ours as they don't use so many spices, whereas the Lebanese use all sorts of different plants and herbs.'

When talking about specific ingredients or recipes, Latifa expresses herself with absolute authority: 'With tagines, you need to find a vegetable that suits the type of meat, and then the spices that suit both. I walk down the street, smell what people are cooking and know exactly what technique they are using as our combinations are so precise. Even the way you cut an onion for each dish is important.' Mention a type of meat, a *coquelet* (a young cockerel), for example, and she responds immediately: 'Oh that's very good stuffed with almonds crushed with raisins, icing sugar, cinnamon and rice.' Like the famed *maallem* (master craftsmen) of Fez, who know dozens of intricate mosaic or plaster patterns by heart, Latifa's sense of gastronomic balance seems to come from deep within her. Her attention to detail is impressive. She is one of the few Moroccan housewives to still make the *smen* (clarified butter – see page 187) that imparts a slightly sharp flavour and unctuousness to dishes like couscous. She even prepares her own spices. Just before cooking a dish, for example, she will grind coriander seeds in a coffee grinder to make an incredibly fragrant powder.

Latifa passed this knowledge of food and cooking on to her sons. 'I have one son and grandchildren here in Fez, another in Paris and Anas in El Jdida,' she says. 'They all know how to cook – I taught them. It's important for men to know how to get by, even if they don't cook often.' Her decisiveness returns again and again: 'Cooking? There's no secret, you just have to get on with it! I never throw anything away and keep all the leftovers to make a gratin or pie using an easy pastry. You just need to know the basics. I had to learn from my aunt, the wife of an uncle, as my mother was an only daughter and so very spoilt that she never lifted a finger! She only knew how to give orders but it's

obviously kept her going – she's now 95! At one point I worked at the Royal Academy in Rabat where we received dignitaries from all over the world – including the first man on the moon, Neil Armstrong! I don't speak English and he didn't speak French, but we understood each other well. We drank coffee and talked a lot.'

You can well believe this, looking at this chic, mature woman in Western clothes with her thick, glossy hair, penetrating eyes and warm, confident manner. Latifa's attitude also works wonders when she shops, as most of the shopkeepers know and respect her and her family, indeed in some cases they are closely related. 'My great-grandfather was a pretty eminent noble in Fez, and it was he who banned the slave market here. He said they were human beings and no human being should be treated like that,' she says.

Laila listens intently to her mother-in-law, nodding in agreement with a big smile. She herself is not a Fassi; she went to university in Marrakech and is now happy living in El Jdida, which is near her own family home. Although superficially more traditional than her mother-in-law (she wears a headscarf and *djellaba* in the presence of any man other than her husband, brothers or father), Laila is charming and easy-going – except when it comes to supervising her tagine. Then her sense of perfection sweeps through the kitchen and you know that both these ladies are of the same ilk. The result is a succession of sumptuous dishes fit for the erstwhile grandees of Fez.

Khoubz   Moroccan flatbread

The method of making the dough for *khoubz* and for *m'simen* (below) is identical and demands intense physical input – there's no slacking in a Fassi kitchen. The bread stays fresh for about 24 hours. Moroccans call it 'our knife and fork', as it is used to pick up food as well as to mop up sauces.

makes 2 medium-sized round loaves

500g (1lb 2oz) flour, half white and half wholemeal
large pinch of salt
1 heaped tbsp easy-blend dried yeast mixed with a little tepid water
about 250ml (9fl oz) water
1 tbsp sesame seeds (optional)

1 - In a large bowl, mix together the flour and salt. Gradually add the yeast mixture and most of the water to form a sticky dough. Knead vigorously on an oiled work surface for about 15 minutes, until elastic and smooth. Work the sesame seeds into the dough, if desired.

2 - Make two large balls, roll them out, then flatten to 1cm (½in) thick. Cover with a damp cloth and leave to rise for 1 hour in a warm place. Preheat the oven to 190°C/375°F/Gas mark 5.

3 - Prick each round of dough with a fork and bake in the preheated oven for 20–30 minutes.

M'simen   Square pancakes

These soft yet crisp square pancakes make great snacks, stuffed with anything from minced meat to fresh white cheese or canned tuna fish. They come into their own during Ramadan when they are devoured at sunset. They are also delicious for breakfast served warm straight from the frying pan then dipped in dark, unrefined honey.

serves 6 (about 10–15 pancakes)

500g (1lb 2oz) flour, half white and half wholemeal
large pinch of salt
a little tepid water
about 250ml (9fl oz) water
4–5 tbsp vegetable oil, plus extra for frying
50g (1¾oz) salted butter, softened

1 - In a large bowl, mix together the flour and salt. Gradually add the water to form a sticky dough. Knead vigorously on an oiled work surface for about 15 minutes, until elastic and smooth.

2 - Make small balls by squeezing the dough in your greased fist so that it balloons above your hand into spheres about the size of a large walnut, or 5–6cm (2–2½in) in diameter. One by one, lightly coat the balls with vegetable oil, then flatten and stretch each one to make a thin

rectangle. Rub the surface with butter, sprinkle with a little flour, fold in the two ends to meet in the centre, then fold in the two sides to get a square. Flatten a little more, maintaining the square shape, then put aside for about 10 minutes.

3 - Heat a little oil in a frying pan over a high heat until it is smoking. Lay the squares one by one in the oil and cook for about 1 minute, then turn over, drizzle a little hot oil over the upper side and cook for another minute. Both sides should be a mottled golden brown. Transfer the pancakes to paper towels to drain off the excess oil, and serve immediately.

Salade d'olives et citrons   Lemon and olive salad

This salad is certainly piquant, due to the sharp lemon flavour backed up by the olives. It's a wake-up starter and needs to be accompanied by something quieter from the vast choice of Fassi salads.

serves 4

2 large lemons, peeled and pith removed

salt

leaves from a bunch of flat leaf parsley, finely chopped

1 tsp sweet paprika

pinch of chilli powder

½ tsp ground cumin (see page 186)

14 purple and black olives, pitted

salt, to taste

2 tbsp extra-virgin olive oil

1 - Submerge the lemons in a bowl of salted water and set aside for about 20 minutes. In another bowl, mix the parsley and spices. Add the olives, salt and olive oil, and stir together.

2 - Drain and halve the lemons. Squeeze out the juice and set it aside. Cut the lemons to olive-sized pieces, remove the pips, and add to the other ingredients. Pour over half the juice and serve.

Loubia   White bean stew

Countless versions of this tasty lunch dish are made at little backstreet eateries in the Fez medina.

serves 4

2 plump, juicy tomatoes

250g (9oz) dried white beans (such as haricot), soaked overnight, drained and rinsed

1 onion, peeled and very finely chopped

2–3 garlic cloves, peeled and crushed

1 tbsp tomato purée, diluted in a little water

leaves from ½ bunch of flat leaf parsley, finely chopped

1 tsp sweet paprika

1 tsp ground ginger

2 tbsp olive oil

1 bay leaf

salt and ground black pepper, to taste

1 - Make a cross at the base of each tomato and plunge them into boiling water for 30 seconds. Transfer to cold water. Drain and remove the loosened skins. Grate the tomatoes.

2 - Put all the ingredients together in a pan with enough water to cover. Simmer gently for 40–50 minutes, or until the beans are cooked through. Adjust salt and pepper, if necessary.

Couscous m'hassel   Sweet chicken couscous

This very ancient Fassi recipe never dies and is just as good with lamb. The sweet onion and raisins blend well and are offset by the golden steaming couscous.

serves 6

vegetable oil for frying, plus 2–3 tbsp for the couscous
1kg (2lb 4oz) onions, peeled and sliced
3 tsp crushed saffron
3 tsp ground ginger
3 tsp ground black pepper
500g (1lb 2oz) raisins
3 tsp ground cinnamon
1–2 tbsp granulated sugar
1½kg (3lb 5oz) chicken pieces
750g (1lb 10oz) couscous
50ml (2fl oz) water
about 100g (3½oz) salted butter
150g (5½oz) toasted almonds (see page 186), to garnish

1 - Heat the vegetable oil in a frying pan and fry the onion and 1 tsp each of the spices (except for the cinnamon) over a low heat until the onion is soft. Add the raisins, 1 tsp cinnamon and the sugar. Cook over a medium heat for 10–15 minutes, stirring occasionally. Set aside to allow the flavours to meld.

2 - Sprinkle the chicken with the remaining spices (saffron, ginger, black pepper and cinnamon) and cook in a steamer, covered, for about 1 hour, or until the chicken is cooked through.

3 - To cook the couscous, follow the instructions on page 186.

4 - Arrange the chicken pieces over the top of the cooked couscous, pour over the onion and raisin mixture, then garnish with a sprinkling of toasted almonds before serving.

Couscous aux sept légumes   Seven-vegetable couscous

Sumptuous, harmonious and with a melt-in-the-mouth quality, the seven-vegetable couscous made in Latifa's household is one of the best you will ever eat. The vegetables must be carefully monitored so they are neither soggy nor crunchy. One of her secrets is homemade *smen* (clarified butter – see page 187), which keeps the couscous grain moist and full of flavour. Salted butter is a good alternative.

serves 4–6

1kg (2lb 4oz) boned shoulder of lamb, cut into large chunks
2 tsp ground ginger
2 tsp yellow-orange colouring, or turmeric (optional)
4–5 tsp ground black pepper
salt, to taste
350ml (12fl oz) vegetable oil
4–5 onions, peeled and sliced
3kg (6lb 8oz) mixed vegetables, such as carrots, turnips, squash or pumpkin, courgettes,
    white cabbage and tomatoes (six types of vegetable in total)
750g (1lb 10oz) couscous
50ml (2fl oz) water
3–4 tbsp vegetable oil
about 100g (3½oz) salted butter

1 - Put the lamb, ginger, colouring or turmeric (if using), seasoning and oil in a large cooking pan or pressure cooker. Stir, then cover with water. Cook over a medium heat for about 1½ hours or in a pressure cooker for 45 minutes, or until the lamb is cooked through.

2 - Meanwhile, prepare the vegetables. Trim and peel the carrots and turnips; trim, peel and deseed the squash or pumpkin; and trim the courgettes. Cut the carrots widthways into halves or thirds. Cut the turnips and squash or pumpkin into equal-sized chunks. Cut the courgettes into halves or thirds. Cut the cabbage into quarters, removing the tough core. Cut the tomatoes in half. Add the vegetables to a large saucepan of boiling salted water in order of cooking time: carrots and turnips first, then the cabbage, courgettes, squash or pumpkin, and tomatoes. Cover and simmer for 20 minutes. Drain.

3 - Meanwhile, to cook the couscous, follow the instructions on page 186.

4 - Spoon the lamb over the cooked couscous and arrange the vegetables around the sides.

Tajine aux sept légumes   Vegetarian tagine

Tagine is based on the principle of ultra-slow cooked meat, but a vegetarian version, using whatever vegetables are in season, is occasionally made for a light supper.

serves 4

> **3–4kg (6lb 8oz–8lb 13oz) mixed vegetables, such as onions, courgettes, carrots, turnips, potatoes, green beans and peas (seven types of vegetable in total)**
>
> **3 tbsp vegetable oil**
>
> **2 tsp ground ginger**
>
> **2 tsp ground black pepper**
>
> **salt, to taste**
>
> **2 tbsp tomato purée, diluted in a little water**
>
> **leaves from a bunch of flat leaf parsley, finely chopped**
>
> **50ml (2fl oz) water**
>
> **200g (7oz) raisins, soaked in water, drained**
>
> **2–3 tsp ground cinnamon, or to taste**

1 - Peel and thickly slice the onions. Trim the courgettes, trim and peel the carrots and turnips, peel or scrub the potatoes, and roughly chop all these into medium-sized chunks. Top and tail the green beans.

2 - Heat the vegetable oil in a large, deep saucepan and add the mixed vegetables, ginger, pepper, salt, tomato purée and chopped parsley, then add half the water. Cover and cook over a low heat for about 30 minutes, adding the remaining water as necessary, plus extra if needed. Add the raisins and cinnamon towards the end of the cooking time.

Tajine aux pruneaux et abricots
Prune and apricot tagine

This is ambrosial stuff, straight from the gods. The sugar is the key: too much and it's inedible, too little and it loses its sweet lusciousness. The other surprise is the walnuts, which break through the sweetness. Laila is the expert in making this dish, and she is as fanatical about its presentation as she is about the reduction of the sauce and the final balance of spices.

serves 4–6

250ml (9fl oz) vegetable oil
pinch of salt
1 tbsp salted butter, melted
3 tsp freshly ground coriander seeds
3 tsp ground ginger
3 tsp ground black pepper
½ tsp yellow-orange colouring, or
    turmeric (optional)
750g–1kg (1lb 10oz–2lb 4oz) shoulder of
    lamb, cut into large chunks
4–5 garlic cloves, peeled and crushed
2 tbsp finely chopped coriander and flat
    leaf parsley leaves

2–3 tbsp water
2 large onions, peeled and diced
500g (1lb 2oz) pitted prunes, soaked
350g (12oz) dried, pitted apricots, soaked
pinch of ground cinnamon
3–6 tbsp caster sugar
large knob of butter
1 tbsp rose water
1 cinnamon stick

to garnish:
15–20 walnut halves
handful of sesame seeds

1 - In a large bowl, mix the oil, salt, butter, spices and colouring or turmeric (if using). Add the lamb pieces and turn to coat. Allow to marinate in the refrigerator for 1 hour.

2 - Transfer the lamb to a pressure cooker or a large, deep saucepan. Cook over a high heat, stirring continuously if using a saucepan, for a few minutes. Add the garlic and herbs. Keep the meat moving around in the pan, then add the water, cover and simmer hard for another 10 minutes.

3 - Add the onions and more water, if necessary, and cook, covered, for a further 20 minutes. Cover the lamb with water and simmer, covered, until the meat is cooked through. This will take about 45 minutes in a pressure cooker, and about 1½ hours in a saucepan.

4 - Meanwhile, prepare the prunes and apricots. Drain the soaked prunes and put them in a saucepan of water to simmer, covered, for 20–30 minutes, or until they are soft and swollen and the water has reduced down slightly. Add the cinnamon and several tablespoons of sugar, according to taste, then stir in the butter to add brilliance, followed by the rose water. Shake the pan to settle the ingredients and stir carefully so as not to break up the prunes. Simmer over a very low heat for about 15 minutes. Prepare the apricots in the same way, minus the butter and rose water, and replacing the ground cinnamon with a cinnamon stick broken into the pan.

5 - When the lamb is cooked through, transfer to a wide platter. Arrange the prunes and apricots over the lamb, then lay half a walnut on each apricot. Pour the meat sauce around the edge and garnish with a sprinkling of sesame seeds.

Tajine aux coings (k'dra)   Quince and lamb tagine

If you can get hold of some quinces, this *k'dra* makes an unusual dish and its combination of fruit and meat provides a perfect harmony of textures. If quinces are unavailable, replace them with pears, which can be caramelized a little before adding them to the sauce by frying them in a pan with a large knob of butter and a tablespoonful of sugar.

serves 6

2–3 tbsp vegetable oil
1kg (2lb 4oz) shoulder of lamb, cut into large chunks
2 onions, peeled and diced
1 tsp ground ginger
1 cinnamon stick, broken in half
pinch of saffron, crumbled
bunch of flat leaf parsley, tied up
bunch of coriander, tied up
pinch of salt
1 heaped tsp ground black pepper
1kg (2lb 4oz) quinces, unpeeled, halved or quartered, and deseeded

1 - Heat the oil in a large, deep pan, and add the lamb, half the onion, the spices, herbs, salt and pepper and enough water to cover the ingredients. Cover with a lid and cook on a low–medium heat for about 1–1½ hours or until the meat is tender, checking the water from time to time to ensure it doesn't boil dry.

2 - Remove the meat from the sauce with a slotted spoon and set aside. Put the quince pieces in the sauce. Add the rest of the onion, adjust the salt, if necessary, and add sufficient water to half-fill the pan. Stir and cook for 15–20 minutes or until the quince is soft and cooked through. Some pieces will cook faster than others, so remove them with a slotted spoon when they are ready, and set aside. When all the quince is cooked and has been removed, simmer the sauce hard to reduce and thicken.

3 - Just before serving, return the meat to the pan, followed by the quince. Reheat over a low heat, taking care not to crush the quince pieces. When heated through, place the meat pieces in a large, wide dish and arrange the quince on top, then pour the sauce over.

Riz au lait avec raisins   Rice pudding with raisins

This pudding can be sickly-sweet, but Latifa avoids this by including orange zest and fragrant orange-blossom water. It makes great comfort food after a light meal.

serves 6

> **100g (3½oz) short-grain rice, rinsed**
> **500ml (18fl oz) milk**
> **200g (7oz) raisins, soaked in water, drained**
> **2 tsp orange zest, finely grated**
> **salt, to taste**
> **2–3 tbsp granulated sugar, or to taste**
> **1 tbsp orange-blossom water**
> **150g (5½oz) blanched almonds, toasted (see page 186) and coarsely chopped, to decorate**

1 - Put the rice in a saucepan and cover generously with water. Cook until the water has been absorbed. Add the milk, raisins, orange zest, salt and sugar, and bring to the boil, stirring continuously. Add the orange-blossom water.

2 - Cook for about 20 minutes, stirring frequently to prevent the rice from sticking to the bottom of the saucepan, until the milk is absorbed, the mixture has thickened and the rice is soft and swollen. The mixture should still be runny.

3 - Empty the mixture into a small bowl, then chill in a refrigerator. If it thickens too much, stir in some cold milk before serving. Invert onto a plate and sprinkle with chopped almonds.

Kenza Samih

'I REMEMBER MAKING LAMB T'FAYA AND CHICKEN WITH PRESERVED LEMON WAY BACK WHEN I WAS A YOUNG GIRL, AND THEY ARE STILL AMONG MY FAVOURITES.'

Kenza Samih, a large statuesque woman in her early 40s, has such pale skin that it seems almost starved of sunlight. That may not be far from the truth as she has been tucked away in kitchens while working as a professional cook for most of her adult life. Watch her wending her way through the crowds of the shadowy souks of Fez El-Bali and she stands out a mile in her long black *djellaba*, black headscarf, fine-rimmed glasses and big smile, and even more so when accompanied by her pretty teenage daughter, Fatima. Kenza is the brain and hands behind the succulent dishes that emerge from the kitchens of Riad Fès, one of the city's top hotel-restaurants. After working here for over six years, she is now such a fixture that the employees call her Meh Kenza – 'Mother Kenza'. The name Kenza actually means 'treasure' and her culinary prowess is indeed precious.

Nabil, one of the suave waiters in black tunics who works beside Kenza six days a week, describes her affectionately: 'She's usually calm and kind to everyone, but sometimes we have particularly demanding clients who expect to be served dinner immediately. Then you've really got to get out of her way. She kicks off her babouches and steams up and down the kitchen like a train!' Kenza smiles gently as she listens to this and continues to chop steadfastly, piling up vegetables for the numerous little starters that are key specialities of Fassi food. Everything at the riad is made freshly each morning and the rhythm of their preparation is familiar – probably achingly so. Behind her, an entire set of state-of-the-art steel knives sits untouched in their block; she is happy to use a tried-and-true knife with a plastic handle. All that matters is a sharp enough blade and total concentration. This is proof, yet again, of how little Moroccan cookery depends on high-tech equipment. The *batterie de cuisine* in most kitchens is limited to gleaming, well-scrubbed pans, steamers and pressure cookers, with only the occasional sighting of a blender or a microwave.

Kenza's employer, Fouzia Sefrioui, is a slim, elegant woman of the Benzakour family who seems to be always on the go, darting in and out of the kitchen to check up on progress. Many of the traditional recipes that Kenza cooks come from her. 'I married very young,' Fouzia explains. 'Then I learned specific dishes with my mother, who was part Marrakshi, part Fassi. It was unusual to do it that way round. Most families teach their daughters cooking before they marry and in some cases they go off to 'train' in specific dishes with their aunts, as each one has a speciality. When Kenza started here, I was behind her a lot to make sure she did it the way I wanted, but she already knew all the exact sauces for tagines, so I felt very confident.'

One of the trump cards of Riad Fès is its sense of presentation, as the dishes have to fit the ethos of such a design-oriented hotel targeting a hip, cosmopolitan clientele. 'I know we're very demanding about quality here,' continues Fouzia, 'and there are tiny details in the preparation of dishes that other cooks don't bother about, but that we think are important.'

Kenza would probably agree. She says, wryly: 'Moroccan cuisine is so complicated that people go mad!' However, it seems to be second nature to her, as she started to cook when she was 12, learning from her grandmother, who was a professional cook for banquets. 'I remember making t'faya [lamb with caramelized carrots – see page 65] and chicken with preserved lemon way back when I was a young girl, and they are still among my favourites. Not much has changed over the years. At one point I worked in Rabat where I learned a few other dishes, including international ones, but traditional Fassi food remains my favourite. My husband likes fish tagines and lamb with quince or artichokes, so I do my best to make them after work. As I work full time, my daughter does the shopping in Tala'a Kbira every morning when the freshest produce is on sale. It's not far from our house. My son Adil is quite a bit older – he's 26 – and has moved away now. I just hope my daughter marries well and moves out too – out of my way!' she says, laughing. 'She's starting to learn a few dishes now, so there's hope!'

The only concession Kenza makes to European palates is the level of sweetness. 'It's true that we Moroccans love pastries and using sugar in our meat dishes, so we try to change the quantities for foreign tastes. But in the end that is the basis of our cuisine, so you could never take it away.'

As a conscientious and highly talented cook, Kenza is more concerned with preparing bstelas for the evening than with chatting about her cooking methods. She is polite but not loquacious, above all concentrated and contained. Ultimately, all that matters is what is in her cooking pot, and there is absolutely no disputing its quality.

FEZ – SCHIZO CITY

About nine thousand alleyways and cul-de-sacs make up this obstinately medieval city, where the unexpected and the extraordinary lie around nearly every corner. Fez is a textbook case of a classic medina functioning completely separately from the French-built new town. Over there, on what seems like another planet, pink and green neon signs wink from bars, cafés and restaurants beneath modern apartment blocks, and Fassis in Western clothes flock to shop at the giant Acima supermarket. A bottle or two of Moroccan wine may slip into their trolley whereas, in the old town, the strict control of the mosques means alcohol is only available inside the riad-hotels. But if you stay within the medina, its rhythms and mores soon become completely normal.

Born in tandem with Morocco's first Imperial dynasty 1,300 years ago, the medina is virtually unchanged structurally, the only sign of the passage of time being the hefty struts propping up the collapsing walls. In the centre is the massive and prestigious Karaouine University, almost as old as the city itself. In front of its library, catching the light on Place Seffarine, sit giant brass and pewter pans fresh from the smelters' fires. Their clanging workshops line one side of the square, and a backstreet or two, so this open space makes an instant showroom. You could cook a couscous for a hundred in just one of the largest pots. Opposite, through studded cedarwood doors, is a 13th-century *medersa*, or Islamic college, where 70 students currently live, pray and work. On one corner is the city's oldest *hammam*, the steam baths that people visit to revitalize their bodies and souls, while a few doors away you can top up your Moroccan mobile or snap up some Berber earrings. Outside the shop sits an eight-year-old boy selling cigarettes from an upturned crate.

Such a crossroads of contrasts could only exist in Fez. Down a side street specializing in horn utensils is a tiny medieval café. It is minimalist in the extreme, with a floor just one grade up from beaten earth, rickety wooden benches and a large copper *samovar* providing the only sustenance. Then thwack goes the stick on the backside of yet another mule with packages roped high on its back as it stumbles past through the alleyway. This time the boxes contain television sets. They could be for Fez's ceramics salesmen to while away spare moments among their beautifully glazed and patterned bowls and platters, another of the city's great specialities. Or they could be destined for Nougat Alley, a row of little shops displaying pink and white blocks of the sticky sweet, no doubt a hangover from the Muslim Spaniards who fled southern Spain to Fez centuries ago. A still earlier Andalucian influx gave the eastern half of the medina the name Al-Andalus, while the western side was settled by Tunisians from Kairouan, hence the name of the university.

And then there are the *muezzin*, the calls to prayer from some 350 mosques. Few other Islamic cities can rival the intensity of the pre-dawn wail in Fez, recalling centuries of cultural and spiritual pre-eminence. In a crescendo of clashing tones, each call tries to outdo the other, from a tiny one-man mosque to the great Kairouine, with its soaring minaret and green-tiled roofs. The complexity of sound and the striving for perfection seem to epitomize this ancient city.

Tadeffi   Garlic, mint and vermicelli soup

A fortifying, warming soup that is served in winter to heat up the body, and traditionally given to women immediately after childbirth, following the consumption of raw eggs. The flavour is gentle, yet intriguing.

serves 4

1 litre (1¾ pints) water
6 tbsp olive oil
2 heaped tbsp wild dried peppermint
2 tsp dried thyme
pinch of saffron, crumbled
pinch of salt
1 tsp ground black pepper
6–8 garlic cloves, chopped
3 tbsp plain flour, mixed with a little water to form a paste
6 tbsp vermicelli

1 - Heat the water in a saucepan over a medium heat and add the olive oil, peppermint, thyme, saffron, salt, pepper and garlic. Bring to boil, reduce the heat and simmer for 15 minutes.

2 - Add the flour paste and vermicelli and simmer, covered, for a further 45 minutes.

Choufleur m'charmel   Spiced cauliflower

You can make this appetizer as garlicky as suits your taste.

serves 6–8 in a mixture of starters

1 cauliflower, broken into florets
leaves from a bunch of flat leaf parsley, finely chopped
4 garlic cloves, peeled and crushed
1 tsp sweet paprika
½ tsp ground cumin (see page 186)
½–1 tsp harissa (see page 186), or to taste
salt, to taste
about 100ml (3½fl oz) water
1–2 tbsp lemon juice, or to taste
3–6 tbsp extra-virgin olive oil

1 - Put all the ingredients except the lemon juice and olive oil in a large saucepan. Cover and cook over a low heat for about 30 minutes, or until the cauliflower is very soft.

2 - Remove the cauliflower from the saucepan with a slotted spoon, then mash with a fork. Add the lemon juice and olive oil, adjust the seasoning if necessary, and serve at room temperature.

Kouar m'charmel   Cabbage with preserved lemon

An alternative preparation for this starter salad would be to add a tablespoonful of sugar while sautéing at the end to capture the salty-sweet character of Moroccan food.

serves 6–8 in a mixture of starters

1 white cabbage, tough core removed, sliced thinly
100ml (3½fl oz) water
salt
2 tbsp olive oil
1 tsp ground cumin (see page 186)
1 tsp ground black pepper
3 garlic cloves, peeled and crushed
leaves from a small bunch of coriander, finely chopped
1 preserved lemon (see page 187), finely diced

1 - Boil the cabbage in the salted water in a covered saucepan over a medium heat for 20 minutes until soft. Remove from the heat and drain.

2 - Heat the olive oil in a frying pan over a medium heat. Add the cumin, pepper, garlic and coriander and sauté for several minutes. Stir in the lemon. Mix in the cabbage. Serve at room temperature.

Carottes à la cannelle   Cinnamon and orange carrots

A classic sweet salad to prepare the palate for a rich tagine to follow.

serves 6–8 in a mixture of starters

500g (1lb 2oz) cooked carrots
juice of 1 orange
2 tbsp caster sugar
1 tsp cinnamon
pinch of salt
2–3 tsp orange-blossom water, or to taste

1 Put all the ingredients in a blender, blend to a purée and chill for about 1 hour to allow the flavours to amalgamate. Serve chilled, accompanied by other starter salads.

T'faya   Lamb with caramelized carrots

Moist and tender, this superbly flavoured lamb should be almost melt-in-the-mouth once cooked. The caramelized carrots look beautiful and their glistening ribbons add an enigmatic touch to the dish.

serves 4

marinade:
1 tsp ground white pepper
2 tsp ground ginger
½ tsp ground black pepper
1 tsp saffron threads, rubbed between the palms of the hands
2–3 tbsp olive oil
2–3 tbsp water

1kg (2lb 4oz) leg of lamb, cut into large chunks
5 large onions, peeled and roughly chopped
5 garlic cloves, peeled
small bunch of coriander, finely chopped
250ml (9fl oz) water
5–6 tbsp vegetable oil
500g (1lb 2oz) carrots, peeled and sliced lengthways then cut into thin batons
5–6 tbsp caster sugar
100g (3½oz) blanched almonds, toasted (see page 186), to garnish

1 - To make the marinade, mix the spices and olive oil together, then stir in the water. Cover the lamb pieces and leave to marinate for 10–15 minutes, then cook for 20 minutes in a frying pan over a low–medium heat.

2 - In a large bowl, mix together the onion, garlic and coriander then add to the lamb along with the water. Cover and cook for at least 2 hours over a low–medium heat, stirring and checking occasionally to see if more water is needed. If using a pressure cooker, halve the water quantity and cook for 45–60 minutes.

3 - Heat the vegetable oil in a separate saucepan, add the carrots and sugar, cover and cook for 5 minutes over a low heat. Uncover the carrots and continue cooking, stirring frequently while they gradually caramelize. After about 30 minutes the carrot mixture should resemble a very coarse marmalade.

4 - Remove the pieces of lamb from the sauce with a slotted spoon and set aside. Strain the sauce, pushing the onion through the sieve with the back of a spoon. Return the sauce to the pan and cook over a high heat. Check the salt and stir continuously for about 20 minutes to reduce. Return the lamb to the sauce and heat for a few minutes.

5 - Place the lamb on a serving dish, arrange the carrot strips around it and garnish with almonds.

Pastilla   Sweet pigeon pie

This complex dish is the *pièce de résistance* of Fassi cuisine – and by extension of Morocco. When perfectly made, it is a light cloud of crisp pastry and tender meat. The sweetness and delicate pastry hit the taste buds first, followed by the creamy egg and, finally, the mysteriously seasoned pigeon. You can make *pastilla* with chicken but the flavour will suffer, as dark pigeon meat is stronger and more gamey. Another option is guinea fowl. Use the finest, most transparent filo pastry you can find. Kenza prepares individual pies in the morning to be baked in the oven later, but for a dinner party two or three larger pies looks more spectacular.

serves 6

350ml (12fl oz) sunflower oil, plus extra
   for frying
½ tbsp ground cinnamon
1 tsp ground ginger
pinch of saffron
1 tsp ground black pepper
½ tsp ground white pepper
pinch of salt
3 pigeons
2 cinnamon sticks, roughly broken
50g (1¾oz) butter
5 tbsp chopped flat leaf parsley
2 heaped tbsp chopped coriander leaves
5 large onions, peeled and roughly chopped
175ml (6fl oz) water
125g (4½oz) granulated sugar
pinch of cinnamon, or to taste

7 rounds of fine filo pastry, about
   25cm (10in) in diameter
250g (9oz) blanched almonds,
   toasted (see page 186) and
   finely ground
2–3 tbsp sunflower oil
1 beaten egg

egg filling:
10 eggs
pinch of salt
1 tsp sugar
pinch of cinnamon

to decorate:
1 tbsp icing sugar
½ tsp ground cinnamon

1 - In a large bowl, mix the oil, spices (except the cinnamon sticks) and salt. Smother the pigeons with this unctuous sauce.

2 - In a large, deep saucepan, heat a little oil and fry the pigeons quickly on all sides to lightly brown. Add the cinnamon sticks, butter, herbs and onion. Add the water, stir, cover, then cook slowly over a medium heat for about 45 minutes, turning half-way through the cooking time. Check the water from time to time to make sure it doesn't boil dry.

3 - Pierce the thickest part of each pigeon thigh to check that the juices run clear and cook for longer if necessary. When cooked through, remove from the saucepan and set aside. Leave the sauce, uncovered, to simmer slowly and reduce for about 15 minutes. Pour through a strainer, or a sieve with large holes, crushing the onion with the back of a spoon to squeeze it through (alternatively whiz the sauce very briefly in a blender). Return to the heat, add the sugar and an extra pinch of cinnamon powder. Stir continuously until reduced to a thick sauce.

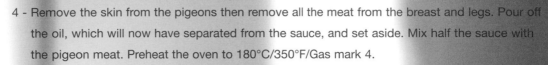

4 - Remove the skin from the pigeons then remove all the meat from the breast and legs. Pour off the oil, which will now have separated from the sauce, and set aside. Mix half the sauce with the pigeon meat. Preheat the oven to 180°C/350°F/Gas mark 4.

5 - To make the egg filling, beat the eggs with the salt, sugar and cinnamon in a large bowl. Heat the set-aside sauce oil in a saucepan over a low heat. Scramble the eggs slowly in the oil until no liquid is left and you have quite a dry consistency. Take the remaining sauce and stir it into the scrambled eggs. Leave both the meat and the scrambled eggs to cool.

6 - On a wide, flat plate, arrange three rounds of pastry so that they overlap slightly and form a large circle. Place another two rounds over the centre to strengthen. Spread the scrambled egg over the centre of the pastry, followed by the pigeon mixture, the ground almonds and sunflower oil. Pull the sides of the pastry together over the top of the filling, then lay two further rounds of pastry over the top and flip the plate over. Stick all the edges together by applying some of the beaten egg with a pastry brush.

7 - Put the pie onto an oiled baking tray and bake in the centre of the preheated oven for about 30 minutes.

8 - Remove the pie from the oven and decorate by sprinkling with icing sugar and criss-crossing with the ground cinnamon.

Mahchi   Stuffed mixed vegetables

It is important that the vegetables are fresh for this delicious light, summery dish. The flavour of paprika and cumin permeates the stuffing and the final dish is wonderfully colourful and cheering.

serves 4–6

10–12 mixed vegetables, such as small courgettes, aubergines, green and red peppers, carrots, small potatoes and onions

stuffing:
750g (1lb 10oz) minced beef
150g (5½oz) cooked long-grain rice
1 large onion, peeled and finely chopped
6 garlic cloves, peeled and crushed
4 tbsp chopped flat leaf parsley
1 tbsp chopped coriander leaves
4 tsp sweet paprika
2 tsp ground cumin (see page 186)
½ tsp chilli pepper
ground black pepper, to taste
salt, to taste
4 tbsp extra-virgin olive oil

sauce:
3–4 tbsp olive oil
1 onion, peeled and grated
5–6 garlic cloves, peeled and roughly chopped
275–325ml (9½–11fl oz) water
2 large tomatoes, halved, deseeded and grated or finely chopped
salt, to taste
½ tsp ground black pepper
3 tsp sweet paprika
2 tbsp finely chopped flat leaf parsley, to garnish

1 - Prepare the vegetables. Trim the courgettes and aubergines. Core and deseed the peppers. Trim and peel the carrots. Scrub or peel the potatoes. Trim and peel the onions. Hollow a cavity in each vegetable with a sharp knife. Set aside.

2 - To make the stuffing, mix together the minced beef, rice, onion, garlic, herbs, spices, salt and olive oil in a bowl. Knead well to form a thick stuffing. Fill each vegetable, packing it tightly with the stuffing, then set aside.

3 - To make the sauce, heat the olive oil in a large, wide saucepan over a medium heat. Add the grated onion and the garlic and stir-fry for about 5 minutes. Add 175ml (6fl oz) water, stir well, then add the tomatoes. Cook to evaporate the liquid and obtain a dense tomato sauce, then add the remaining water, followed by the salt, pepper and paprika. Stir well, part-cover the pan and simmer for about 1 minute.

4 - Place the stuffed vegetables in a large saucepan (try to have each one sitting on its base in the pan) and spoon over the sauce. Cover and cook over a medium heat for 15–25 minutes, removing each vegetable as it is cooked (test for softness by pricking with a skewer or fork) and the beef stuffing is cooked through. Garnish with parsley and serve in a wide, shallow dish.

Tchicha   Barley soup

This is an easy soup to whip up at any time and uses fairly basic ingredients.

serves 4–6

1½ litres (2¾ pints) water
175ml (6fl oz) olive oil
2 onions, peeled and very finely chopped
2 tomatoes, peeled with a vegetable peeler and finely chopped
salt, to taste
1 tsp ground black pepper
200g (7oz) barley
2 tbsp tomato purée
leaves from a bunch of flat leaf parsley, roughly chopped
handful of celery leaves, roughly chopped

1 - Heat the water in a saucepan over a medium heat. Add the olive oil, onion, tomato, salt and pepper. Bring to the boil then add the barley, tomato purée, parsley and celery leaves.
2 - Cover and simmer for 30–40 minutes over a low–medium heat, or until the barley has softened.

Tajine de crevettes   Prawn tagine

The prawns in this hot, garlicky tagine were not traditionally a part of the Moroccan diet. The recipe probably came via the Spanish who colonized northern Morocco and developed the seafood industry around Larache. Be careful not to overcook it, as the prawns easily lose their texture.

serves 4

500g–600g (1lb 2oz–1lb 5oz) cooked, peeled tiger prawns
2 red peppers, finely chopped
1 tsp finely chopped chilli pepper
8 garlic cloves, peeled and crushed
3–4 tbsp finely chopped coriander leaves
8–10 tbsp olive oil
½ tbsp sweet paprika
salt, to taste

1 - Mix all the ingredients together in a bowl and leave to marinate for at least 30 minutes, or longer if possible.
2 - Transfer to a saucepan and cook over a high heat, stirring continuously, for 5–10 minutes. Serve immediately.

Frakh maamar
Pigeon stuffed with couscous, raisins and almonds

Pigeon meat is stronger than chicken and makes this a sumptuous main course, but if pigeon is not available you could use chicken – then it becomes *djaja maamar*. The textural contrasts are a major element in this dish and the sweet golden stuffing wakes up even the most jaded of palates.

serves 4–6

2 large pigeons or 1 chicken, about 1½kg (3lb 5oz)

stuffing:
100g (3½oz) couscous, steamed for 15 minutes, or steeped in just-boiled water for
**   5 minutes until swollen, then broken up with a fork**
75g (2¾oz) blanched almonds, toasted (see page 186) and coarsely chopped
2 tbsp olive oil
125g (4½oz) raisins
3 tsp ground cinnamon
pinch of salt

sauce:
3 tbsp vegetable oil
1 large onion, peeled and very finely chopped
leaves from a bunch of flat leaf parsley, finely chopped
2 tsp ground ginger
pinch of saffron
1 tsp ground black pepper
pinch of salt
about 250–300ml (9–10fl oz) water
75g (2¾oz) salted butter

1 - In a bowl, mix the stuffing ingredients together to form a thick consistency, then fill the cavity of the pigeons (or the chicken), packing it in well. Tuck the skin in to cover the stuffing, cross the legs and then tie up or, for the chicken, tie the legs together tightly with string.

2 - To make the sauce, heat the olive oil in a large saucepan, add the onion, parsley, spices and salt. Add the pigeons or chicken and sufficient water to cover. Stir, and bring to the boil. Add the butter, then reduce to a medium heat and simmer, covered, for 30–40 minutes for the pigeons or 40–50 minutes for the chicken, turning occasionally and adding more water if necessary. Meanwhile, preheat the oven to 220°C/425°F/Gas mark 7.

3 - Remove the pigeons or chicken from the liquid and place in a greased ovenproof dish. Roast for 20–30 minutes in the preheated oven. Pierce the thickest part of the thigh to check that the juices run clear and cook for longer if necessary. Meanwhile, stir the sauce over the heat to reduce. Serve the pigeons or chicken cloaked in the sauce, on a wide platter.

Khizou mahkouk   Carrot and orange soup

Carrot and orange is a fantastic combination that is common in Tunisian salads. This wonderfully fresh Moroccan soup is a dreamy liquid version, packed with vitamins, and can be eaten either as a starter or as a dessert. It should not be too runny and should retain a granular quality from the carrots. As an alternative to mint, scatter with fresh basil leaves.

serves 6

500g (1lb 2oz) carrots, peeled and grated
pinch of salt
2 tbsp caster sugar
4 tbsp orange-blossom water
500ml (18fl oz) orange juice

to decorate:
6 large mint leaves
1–2 tsp icing sugar

1 - Whiz the carrots, salt, sugar and orange-blossom water in a blender for about 1 minute, or until nearly smooth, but still slightly granular. Add the orange juice and whiz again, very briefly, to blend. Leave the mixture in the refrigerator for at least 2 hours to intensify the flavours.

2 - Serve the chilled soup in individual bowls each decorated with a mint leaf and sprinkled with icing sugar.

Khadouj Sentwi

'COOKING IS INGRAINED IN ME AND SUCH A HABIT THAT I COULD NEVER STOP DOING IT. I MADE MY FIRST MEAL SINGLE-HANDEDLY WHEN I WAS 14.'

Khadouj is an *éminence grise* of Fassi cuisine. Now 60, she has been cooking ever since she stood at her mother's elbow in the family kitchen in Fez medina – watching her make pastry, turn over the couscous, or prepare a tagine for an ever-multiplying family. 'I was always curious and loved sticking my hands in the food and tasting it,' she recalls. 'The first dish I helped my mother with was a lamb and quince tagine. I must have been about ten at the time. I still love that balance of the quince confit made with sugar and cinnamon and cooked with lamb.' She could not be a more unadulterated source of Fassi culinary knowledge. Her food is untouched by any outside influence; in all those years, she has never set foot outside the city and has always lived in the medina. Ask her if she has any Berber blood, like so many Moroccans, and she is vehement: 'No, no! I'm Fassi, like my parents and ancestors.'

Khadouj's home is a few minutes' steep walk uphill from the food market at Rcif, where she does all her shopping. 'I buy absolutely everything there,' she says. 'It might be cheaper elsewhere but here you can rely on the quality, and after so many years I know all the shopkeepers.' This ancient quarter of Fez has a strong village atmosphere, and Khadouj is one of its fixtures. What sets her apart from the other Fassi housewives filling their bags is that she has worked for 28 years at one of the foremost traditional restaurants in Fez, Dar El Ghalia. Here she added to her repertoire the recipes of the Lebbars, one of the city's grand old families.

Today, although officially retired, Khadouj still prepares all the important feasts for religious festivals, weddings or births for her four children and 11 grandchildren. 'Cooking is ingrained in me, and such a habit that I could never stop doing it. I made my first family meal single-handedly when I was 14, then I married at 15 and had my first child at 16. I had five more children, one after the other – two have since died – and I had my hands full bringing up and feeding them all. Then, when I was 25, my husband died suddenly. That was when I started working for Monsieur and Madame Lebbar.'

Despite the tragedies in her life, Khadouj's story is uplifting as it proves that even a woman from a modest background can rise above circumstances and find a respected place in this male-oriented society. She says: 'When I started at El Ghalia, I learned so much more about cooking and soon realized I had a skill and could do something with my life.' She considers herself lucky to have found an employer like Omar Lebbar. 'I respect him and have a lot of affection for him. He's a very generous man and good towards his employees.' Her warmth is genuine, like everything else about Khadouj.

Although her long, somewhat mournful face often masks this, when she is relaxed and not cooking, her mischievous side erupts in the form of obscure jokes and expressive rolls of her eyes.

Her temper is, nonetheless, legendary at El Ghalia, where she was the iron lady of the kitchen as well as being 'the mother of everyone', as one employee whispers. Omar Lebbar himself remembers the power of her presence. 'When she worked here you really knew it!' he says. 'She has a very strong personality and temperament and was very authoritarian in the kitchen. She would also involve herself in the service and presentation of each dish with a perfectionist's eye for detail. If a waiter was slow in taking a hot dish to a table, he would really hear about it!' That same power obviously still has an effect on him, as he adds: 'But I have immense respect for her. She's a very intelligent woman.'

With age, Khadouj has obviously softened. Her face lights up when she talks about the imminent Muslim festival. 'Ramadan is the big family moment when we cook and eat most – although we're fasting during the day for the entire 30 days. We can't even drink and that's really difficult, especially when it's hot. Every evening after sunset and the fourth prayer, we have a huge dinner. It has to be different every day – the main dish can be anything based on fish, chicken or meat. We also eat far too many pastries! And no, I don't make them as you can buy very good ones from the shops in Bab Sensla. Then, just before sunrise we start the day with *harira*, *briouats* [pastries], boiled eggs, fresh white cheese and *baghrira* [a spongy pancake 'of a thousand holes'].'

Although a traditionalist, Khadouj admits to having adopted a few short cuts. 'I used to prepare all my spices but now I buy them from the market. I know where to get the good ones. The only spice I prepare myself is *ras-el-hanout* to get exactly the right balance.' Watching her operate behind the pots and pans, like the conductor of an orchestra, it is obvious that her sense of timing and method remain perfect: little can replace such long years of hard-won experience.

FEZ: DOWN BY THE DOCKS

Rcif market in Fez straggles along a half-covered alleyway below street level, like a subterranean labyrinth bisecting the two historic halves of the medina. Its deep shadows, trellis patterns and cool air feel far removed from the harsh sunshine bouncing off the biscuit-coloured walls above. Rcif is not like Souk Attarine, the intoxicating parade of scents and spice at the more touristy top of the hill, where narrow donkey- and mule-packed lanes make up the inner medina. This more functional market lies at the base of the hill, next to an open plaza that buzzes with buses and *petits taxis*. Modern ease of access makes it a magnet for the more practical members of the food-obsessed population.

Rcif actually means 'docks', pointing to the area's original role. Just behind the market's monumental gateway, a 1,000-year-old bridge crosses the former riverbed of the Oued Fez, now filled with garbage and scavenging cats, and typical of Morocco's less picture-postcard underbelly. The river was crucial to the city's early development. Water was said to be God's gift to Fez and it was once pumped from here through a network of canals to houses, mosques, *hammams*, tanneries and gardens. This ingenious piece of medieval engineering also fed around 60 public fountains, each one a tiled work of art, while the cool patios of magnificent riads had their own wells.

Today Rcif market greets shoppers with a spectacular assault of gleaming produce from the city's environs. Depending on the season, these could be golden grapes from Lemta, dark wild cherries from Sefrou, barrowloads of thirst-quenching prickly pears sliced open and eaten on the spot, knobbly oranges from the orchards around Meknes, zingy, crimson arbutus berries, walnuts from the Rif mountains and barrows of superbly imperfect seasonal vegetables, all naturally organic.

Other stalls stack up plastic buckets containing mutton fat and *khlii*, a sun-dried, spiced meat designed as a winter fallback. Then there is a camel head announcing a butcher's purple-coloured camel meat; tiny groceries with sugar loaves wrapped in blue paper and sacks of golden semolina; recycled bottles filled with rose water; the patisserie stalls of Bab Sensla; snail-soup sellers; fishmongers who run out of their silvery Atlantic catch within hours; freshly made yogurt sold for one dirham a glass; creamy white cheeses; and mountains of shiny olives propped up on plastic plates. Beside this bounty, women expertly make *warka*, the gossamer-thin pastry used in pastillas and pastries: after pouring batter over a griddle, they whip the half-cooked sheet through the air then drape it over a heated iron surface to solidify, in yet another masterful, centuries-old Fassi art. Then there's the chicken seller who weighs the live chicken of your choice before having it killed, plucked, trussed and ready to go 15 minutes later. Time may be elastic here, but as far as food is concerned nothing – fish, camel or fowl – hangs around for long.

Serrouda   Chickpeas in tomato and herb sauce

This is one of the traditional Fassi recipes that Khadouj revived for El Ghalia. It is served as one of four or five small starters. The ingredients are beautifully amalgamated with a sweet edge from the onions.

serves 6–8 in a mixture of starters

500g (1lb 2oz) dried chickpeas, soaked overnight, drained and rinsed

500g (1lb 2oz) onions, peeled and sliced

3 plump, juicy tomatoes, diced

pinch of saffron

leaves from a small bunch of flat leaf parsley, finely chopped

2–3 tbsp extra-virgin olive oil

salt and ground black pepper, to taste

1 - Rub the soaked chickpeas with your fingers on a board to remove the skins. Discard the skins.

2 - Put the chickpeas together with the remaining ingredients into a saucepan or pressure cooker. Mix, then add enough water to cover. Simmer for 1 hour in the saucepan or 30 minutes in the pressure cooker, or until the chickpeas are cooked through. Adjust seasoning, if necessary, then serve warm.

Lentilles aux tomates et paprika
Lentils with tomatoes and paprika

Lentils have a delightfully earthy flavour and harmonize easily with tomatoes and paprika. For extra bite, add crushed chilli pepper, to taste.

serves 6–8 in a mixture of starters

250g (9oz) green or brown lentils

2 large tomatoes, chopped

2 large onions, peeled and sliced

1 heaped tsp sweet paprika

salt, to taste

1 tsp ground black pepper

1 - In a saucepan or pressure cooker, boil the lentils in water for about 15 minutes. Drain and replace the water, covering the lentils, then add the tomatoes, onion, sweet paprika, salt and pepper.

2 - Cook for an additional 30 minutes in the saucepan or 15 minutes in the pressure cooker, until the lentils are cooked through.

Tomates au miel   Honeyed tomatoes

This confit is like a sweet tomato jam, very dense and sugary. It can be stored in a sealed jar in the refrigerator and spooned out occasionally. Beware of eating too much as it is very rich. Like all such little starters, it is eaten with four or five others and dipped into with a fork or flatbread.

serves 4–6 in a mixture of starters
   2kg (4lb 8oz) tomatoes
   175ml (6fl oz) vegetable oil
   1 tsp cinnamon
   90ml (3fl oz) caster sugar
   90ml (3fl oz) honey
   salt, to taste

1 – Make a cross at the base of each tomato and plunge them into boiling water for 30 seconds. Transfer to cold water. Drain and remove the loosened skins. Halve, remove the juice and seeds, dice, then place in a wide pan with a drizzle of the vegetable oil. Stir continuously over a low heat until the mixture starts to simmer, then add the rest of the oil, the cinnamon, sugar and honey.

2 - Simmer for 1–1½ hours, stirring occasionally, until the mixture has reduced right down, there is no liquid left and only a film of oil remains on the surface.

Batata heloua   Sweet potato with raisins

This typically salty-sweet combination makes an unusual vegetable starter.

serves 6–8 in a mixture of starters
   2 tbsp vegetable oil
   2 large onions, peeled and sliced
   pinch of salt
   pinch of saffron
   ground black pepper, to taste
   250ml (9fl oz) water
   1kg (2lb 4oz) sweet potatoes, peeled and cut into large chunks
   150g–200g (5½–7oz) raisins
   leaves of a bunch of flat leaf parsley, finely chopped, to garnish

1 – Heat the vegetable oil in a saucepan and add the onion, salt, saffron, pepper and water. Bring to the boil, reduce the heat and simmer for 20 minutes.

2 – Add the sweet potatoes and raisins, stir, then cover and cook over a medium heat for about 40 minutes. Garnish with the chopped parsley and serve warm.

Poivrons grillés aux citrons confits
Grilled peppers with lemon confit

This is a delicious, fresh starter that will awaken the taste buds. The plastic bag technique used for removing the skin of the peppers works well, as the heat trapped inside the bag softens their skins.

serves 6–8 in a mixture of starters

1kg (2lb 4oz) green peppers, halved, cored and deseeded

1 tsp ground cumin (see page 186)

2–3 garlic cloves, peeled and crushed

leaves from a bunch of flat leaf parsley, finely chopped

1 preserved lemon (see page 187), finely sliced

salt, to taste

1 - Preheat the oven to 190°C/375°F/Gas mark 5. Roast the peppers for 30–45 minutes, or until soft. Remove from the oven and transfer to a polythene bag. Leave to soften for 15 minutes.

2 - Remove the peppers from the bag, rinse, then remove and discard the charred, outer skin.

3 - Finely chop the skinned peppers, add the cumin, garlic, parsley and preserved lemon. Stir well together, season with salt and serve.

Harira   Chickpea soup

Warming and comforting, this is the soup that traditionally breaks the fast at sunset during Ramadan, and most Moroccans love it. Transform it into a *shorba Fassia* (Fez soup) by adding two or more vegetables such as potatoes and carrots, and a handful of vermicelli in place of the rice and flour.

serves 4–6

250g (9oz) dried chickpeas, soaked overnight, drained and rinsed

1 large onion, peeled and finely sliced

2 large tomatoes, peeled with a vegetable peeler and grated

pinch of saffron

salt and ground black pepper, to taste

100g (3½oz) cooked rice

50g (1¾oz) plain flour mixed with a little water to make a paste

bunch of coriander, finely chopped

1 celery heart

1 - Place the chickpeas, onion, tomatoes, saffron, salt and pepper in a large saucepan with enough water to cover the ingredients. Place over a medium heat, stir together and cover with a lid, then simmer hard for about 30 minutes.

2 - Add the remaining ingredients, stir well, check the seasoning, and add more water if necessary. Simmer, covered, for a further 30 minutes. Remove the celery heart before serving.

Poulet m'charmel   Lemon chicken with coriander and olives

When the balance is just right, this dish is quite exquisite. Many similar recipes suggest cooking the olives, but this makes it overly bitter. Here, they complement the tartness of the lemon perfectly by being added at the end.

serves 4–5

2 large onions, peeled and finely chopped

3–4 garlic cloves, peeled and crushed

bunch of coriander, finely chopped

leaves from a bunch of flat leaf parsley, finely chopped

1 tsp ground ginger

1 tsp ground cumin (see page 186)

1 tsp ground black pepper

salt, to taste

juice of 2 lemons

175ml (6fl oz) olive oil

about 350 ml (12fl oz) water

1 chicken, about 1½kg (3lb 5oz), left whole or cut into quarters if serving 4 and into
eighths if serving more

to garnish:
1 preserved lemon (see page 187), finely sliced
150g (5½oz) soft green or purple olives

1 - In a large bowl, mix together the onion, garlic, half the coriander and parsley, the spices, salt, half the lemon juice and the olive oil. Dilute with the water to make a sauce.

2 - Rub some of the sauce into the cavity and over the outside of the whole chicken, or over the chicken pieces, then place the chicken in a large cooking pan. Pour the rest of the mixture around the meat, cover and simmer over a medium heat for 1–1¼ hours if using a whole chicken, or 30–45 minutes if using chicken pieces (the breast will cook quicker than the dark meat), turning occasionally and adding more water if necessary.

3 - To ensure that the chicken is cooked through, pierce the thickest part of the thigh to check that the juices run clear and cook for longer if necessary. Add the remaining coriander and parsley and pour over the remaining lemon juice. Leave to simmer hard for a few more minutes to thicken the sauce.

4 - Arrange the chicken on a dish and garnish with slices of preserved lemon and the olives.

Hout khoudra   Marinated fish with vegetables

Although Fez is quite a way from the coast, fish figures prominently in its cuisine and fresh sardines
are a regular street snack. The fish comes by refrigerated truck from Agadir and Larache daily, so
housewives have to take pot luck (literally!). Here, you could use fish such as turbot, sea bream or
sea bass. The finished dish looks very fresh and decorative.

serves 6–8

1 tsp ground cumin (see page 186)
1 tsp sweet paprika
4–5 garlic cloves, peeled and crushed
bunch of coriander, finely chopped
juice of 1 lemon
4 tbsp white wine vinegar
2 tbsp water
1–2 large fish (about 1½–2kg/3lb 5oz–4lb 8oz in total), scaled, gutted and cleaned,
**   heads kept on**
olive oil, to drizzle
3–4 large carrots, peeled and thickly sliced in rounds
4 large tomatoes, sliced
2–3 green peppers, cored, deseeded and sliced into rounds
500g (1lb 2oz) potatoes, peeled and thinly sliced

1 - Mix the spices, garlic, coriander, lemon juice and vinegar together in a bowl with the water to
     create a liquid *chermoula* paste. Put half the mixture inside the fish and smear most of the rest
     over the body, rubbing it in well. Drizzle with a little olive oil so that the fish is well lubricated.
     Leave for 15 minutes to marinate. Preheat the oven to 190°C/375°F/Gas mark 5.

2 - Arrange the sliced carrots on the bottom of a large, wide, ovenproof pan, then place the fish
     on top. Dilute the remaining *chermoula* with 1–2 tbsp more water and spoon over the fish, then
     arrange the sliced tomatoes and peppers over the top. Drizzle over some more olive oil. Put
     the sliced potatoes around the edge. Pour 1–2 tbsp more water around the edge then place
     the pan over a medium heat and simmer for about 15 minutes.

3 - Put the pan in the preheated oven and cook for 30 minutes, or until the fish and potatoes are
     cooked through. Serve the fish with all the vegetables except the carrots.

Tajine d'agneau aux pruneaux   Lamb and prune tagine

Meltingly sweet in its silken, velvety sauce, this is one of the kings of Fassi tagines, cooked in a classic *m'qualli* sauce. It is rich so should be served as a main course between a light starter and dessert.

serves 4–5

1 tsp ground ginger
1 tsp saffron
salt, to taste
3 large onions, peeled and chopped
2 garlic cloves, peeled and crushed
175ml (6fl oz) olive oil

1kg (2lb 4oz) lamb, such as shoulder,
   cut into large chunks
400g (14oz) pitted prunes
1 tbsp ground cinnamon
2 tbsp granulated sugar
100g (3½oz) blanched almonds,
   toasted (see page 186), to decorate

1 - Mix the ginger, saffron and salt with the onion, garlic and oil. Put in a large saucepan with the lamb and almost cover the meat with water. Cook, covered with a lid, for about 1¼ hours, checking the water from time to time to ensure it doesn't boil dry. Remove the lid to allow the sauce to reduce 10 minutes before the end of cooking time.

2 - Meanwhile, put the prunes into a saucepan, cover with water and simmer hard for 30 minutes. Remove with a slotted spoon, change the water, return the prunes to the heat and add the cinnamon and sugar. Simmer for a further 30 minutes.

3 - When the lamb is cooked, remove from the saucepan and place in a serving dish. Surround with the prunes and spoon the meat sauce over the top. Decorate with the almonds.

Poulet m'bakhbar   Steamed and stuffed chicken

The chicken used in this recipe should be top-quality organic as the flavour and texture of the meat is what makes it so good. This dish has no added oil and is packed with flavour, so is perfect for dieters.

serves 4

    1 organic chicken, about 1½kg (3lb 5oz), with giblets

    1 tsp ground ginger

    1 tsp ground cumin (see page 186)

    1 tsp sweet paprika

    1 tsp ground black pepper

    pinch of salt

    leaves from ½ bunch coriander, finely chopped

    125g (4½oz) cooked long-grain rice

    2 large onions, peeled and finely chopped

    2–3 garlic cloves, peeled and crushed

    1 tbsp olive oil (optional), plus extra for greasing

    about 350ml (12fl oz) water

1 - Remove the liver from the chicken and chop. In a bowl, combine the spices, salt, coriander, chicken liver, rice, onion and garlic with 1–2 tbsp water and the olive oil (if using) to make an unctuous stuffing. Pack the cavity of the chicken with the stuffing, then sew it up with a needle and thick thread or tie the legs together, pulling the skin over the stuffing and tucking it in.

2 - Place the chicken in a large cooking pan. Pour the water around the meat, cover, and simmer over a medium heat for 1 hour, turning occasionally and adding more water if necessary. Meanwhile, preheat the oven to 190°C/375°F/Gas mark 5.

3 - To ensure that the chicken is cooked through, pierce the thickest part of the thigh to check that the juices run clear and cook for longer if necessary. Remove the chicken from the pan and place in a greased ovenproof dish in the oven for about 10 minutes. This dries the chicken slightly and ensures that the dish is not soggy. Serve immediately.

Shorbat bil looz   Chilled almond milk

This sweet, fragrant drink is imbibed by
the Fassi bourgeoisie on feast days.

serves 4–6

150g (5½oz) caster sugar
200g (7oz) almonds, skinned
250ml (9fl oz) water
1 litre (1¾ pints) full fat milk
3 tbsp orange-blossom water
ice cubes, to serve

1 - Put half the sugar, the almonds and a quarter of the water in a
    blender and whiz. Pour through a fine sieve.
2 - Mix the remaining sugar and water with the milk and orange-
    blossom water, then stir together with the almond mixture.
    Serve in long glasses with ice cubes.

ماء ألبلدي
المختار

Pastilla au lait   Cream pastilla with orange-blossom water

Light as the froth of a daydream, this layered spectacle of alternate creaminess and crisp pastry is a great party piece, although quite fiddly to make. The taste of the orange-blossom water comes through loud and clear, cutting through the sweetness of the cream.

serves 6

vegetable oil, for deep frying
6–9 sheets of filo pastry
250g (9oz) white short-grain rice
2–3 tbsp caster sugar
salt, to taste
125ml (4fl oz) full fat milk
3–4 tbsp orange-blossom water

to decorate:
3–4 tbsp icing sugar
4 tsp ground cinnamon
100g (3½oz) blanched almonds, toasted (see page 186), and coarsely chopped
6 mint sprigs

to serve:
1 orange, peeled and divided into segments
2–3 tbsp bitter orange marmalade, diluted with 1–2 tbsp water

1 - Cut each filo pastry sheet into two or three equal-sized rectangles, depending on the original size of the sheet. Heat a deep frying pan half-filled with vegetable oil over a medium heat and deep-fry the pastry sheets one by one until they are golden and crisp, stacking them with pieces of paper towel placed in between to separate them. Set aside.

2 - Boil the rice in a saucepan of water set over medium heat for 20–30 minutes until soft. Put the rice and a little of its cooking water in a blender and whiz to form a creamy liquid. Place in a bowl, add the sugar and salt, then slowly pour in the milk and orange-blossom water, stirring continuously, to form a thick, paste-like liquid. Transfer to a saucepan and simmer over a low heat for about 10–15 minutes to thicken further until the liquid has a creamy consistency.

3 - Assemble the pastillas at the last minute before serving. Make two or three, depending on the size of the pastry, alternating layers of pastry and cream and using six layers of pastry sandwiched together with cream for each pastilla. Cut the pastillas to give six individual portions. Decorate the top layer of pastry with sifted icing sugar and lines of cinnamon, chopped almond and some mint sprigs. Serve with segments of orange and the diluted marmalade.

TUNIS

تونسي

Dalila Amdouni

Dalila – an earthy turbo-ball of energy and laughter – is the mainstay of the holiday riad of her Parisian employers in the heart of the Tunis medina. This is where she produces dish after aromatic dish that leave every parting guest salivating to return. More often than not she is seconded in the kitchen by Ahmed, her serene husband who doubles as the caretaker. Their setting is a stunning 16th-century courtyard house of lofty ceilings, alcoves and roof terraces that, over the last decade, has evolved into an oasis of refinement. Renovated along purist lines, it acts as a frame to eclectic design elements and rare finds from all over the world – as well as a prolific orange tree (source of the house marmalade), a couple of tortoises, Carthago the cat and a cheerful canary. One of Dalila's greatest talents is to remain sublimely unimpressed by this design obsession – and to merely roll her eyes at a new gadget from Japan or a bowl from Brazil.

Outside the studded yellow door and narrow alleyway lies another world, its rhythms governed by the ear-splitting 8th-century Ez-Zitouna mosque which towers over the covered souks. Here glittery plastic slippers are displayed side by side with handbeaten copper pans, *djellabas*, perfumes and even witches' herbs. Thousands of people push through the main artery daily, oblivious to the glorious concoctions bubbling away in Dalila's kitchen just a few yards away.

Dalila's talents are severely tested all year long as her employers welcome a stream of sophisticated foreign guests, most with extremely fine-tuned palates. Yet, whether from Europe, America or Australia, these cosmopolitan visitors are easily seduced by Dalila and her dishes. Much of this success can be put down to her good humour: 'I laugh a lot – it's the only way, even when my husband and children get on my nerves!' Somehow that laughter permeates her cooking – simple, fresh, generous dishes that are punchy in flavour yet do not take hours to prepare. Above all they can easily be expanded to cope with the impromptu appearance of Tunisian friends at the studded door.

'I first learned to cook from my mother,' explains Dalila, 'and since then I've collected ideas chatting with women friends – we share tips and recipes. I was 15 when my mother first said, "I'll die one day soon so you've got to learn cooking – NOW!". She'd stand over me and hit me if I got it wrong, saying, "You won't find a husband like that!". I remember when I started learning to make bread I burned my arms quite badly on the oven. There were eight of us altogether in the family, four boys and four girls, so we needed a lot of feeding, but my mother still managed to be a great cook. I'm now trying to convince my 15-year-old daughter to learn – though she's doing her best to avoid it!'

Dalila somehow works miracles in a limited space, part of which is open to the sky. She and Ahmed manage most of the preparation on one marble table. They use few gadgets and she'll cook a five-course meal for 20 guests on three gas burners and a large oven at the drop of a *chéchia* – or hat. Dalila's trick is to work sparingly, never wasting space, time or using unnecessary utensils; she'll chop up an ingredient directly over the cooking pan rather than use an extra board and will separate an egg over the bin, chucking the white directly and keeping the yolk in the shell. With no dishwasher, washing up can reach epic proportions, so Dalila is living proof of the validity of washing as you go. It means the kitchen always has an atmosphere of control. Her other trick is to remain calm – and ever smiling.

Partly thanks to the easy attitude of her employers and partly thanks to her temperament, there is no sense of subordination here; Dalila is a mind unto herself who nonetheless always comes up with the goods. It's a long habit as she has been working as a family cook since she was 20 – nearly 30 years in other words. 'I started work with a French family in Carthage – they just let me get on with it. I even took their two children on holiday to the south of France, to Nice and to Marseilles. Yes, I did eat French food but the family kept asking me to prepare Tunisian dishes! Then I got married and worked with a Tunisian lady before I came here.

'Do I get ideas from other people? I'll watch them cooking and pinch some of their combinations of ingredients or methods but there's no single dish that I've copied entirely.

'I use my eyes a lot – I watch carefully, such as when I go to the market. Whether it's the big Marché Central just outside the medina, the smaller one near here or my local one in Carthage, I always do the same thing: I walk around and look. I don't speak much and I hardly touch anything. I can tell when the fish is good by its eyes – they sparkle! I also see the price – that's important. My husband doesn't choose, he just buys anything. We never eat out – I don't like it; I much prefer my own cooking.'

After sunset, Dalila's working day is over and she sets off to her home and two children in Carthage. This is the moment when swallows circle high above the elegant patio with its soaring alcoves, around the neighbouring minaret and over the surrounding labyrinth of the medina. Shutters clatter noisily as the souk closes up, a few last shopkeepers linger to chat, cats slink round corners to nibble at garbage, and Dalila resumes her other life – never far from a cooking pot.

INTO THE TUNIS MEDINA

Nosing around the Fondok El Ghalia – Tunis's central market – is a tantalizingly sensory experience, with enough colour, aromas and texture to set anyone seriously salivating. On display is the whole of the Mediterranean plus a corner of Africa, from mountains of delicate pink rose petals to silvery fish of all dimensions, tentacular octopus, pyramids of deep orange harissa, round white mounds of creamy, fresh cheese, buckets of fragrant mint – and a few heads of sheep in between. Glossy vegetables and plump fruit grown in Cap Bon to the east and in Mejerda, the fertile belt to the west, change with the seasons – nothing is imported. It feels like a land of plenty, despite the fact that half of Tunisia is covered by the Sahara Desert.

In small shops just outside the covered market, you can fill a bottle with unctuous extra-virgin olive oil from Sahel sold straight from the barrel (Tunisia is the largest producer outside Europe – and some even finds its way into Italian bottles). You can also buy orange-blossom honey, sesame seeds, ground or whole almonds, pistachios and pulses from brimming sacks, as well as bags of pickles or gleaming purple, green and black olives. A reassuringly old-fashioned style of shopping ensures that desired quantities are measured out to the gram, proving that in Tunisian homes food is infinitely more varied than the ubiquitous *brik à l'oeuf* – a large triangle of very flaky pastry containing egg – which is force-fed to every tourist.

Recently restored to their former tiled and whitewashed splendour with upgraded facilities for 800 stallholders, the lofty market buildings stand a block east of the Bab Bhar. This triumphal arch crowns the Place de la Victoire and is an emblematic front line between modern Tunis and the 1,400-year-old medina. The former extends eastwards to the sea through open boulevards in 1880s French style; the latter is an enclosed world of shady, narrow lanes of shops and houses punctuated by beautifully tiled mosques, mausoleums, neighbourhood *hammams*, secret patios and North Africa's largest second-hand clothes market. The two cities could not be more different.

Socio-economically advanced (women are far more emancipated than in other North African countries), Tunisia still clings to its French heritage – and that includes baguettes and Danone. French names and words crop up again and again, and even Monoprix has found its niche. Along the Avenue de France pavement cafés serve *oranges pressées* and *cafés crèmes* to young women in jeans as if it were the Boulevard Saint-Germain. Then there is the neighbourly influence of Italy, immediately across the sea: for Tunisians, tomato sauce is 'salsa', and the central market has a vast choice of fresh pasta backed up by ricotta, Parmesan and Sicilian cheeses.

The atmosphere changes radically in the medina. Cafés around the perimeter serve hookah pipes and syrupy mint tea to a predominantly male clientele, while inside the maze of flaking alleyways you enter a world of miauling cats, bustling souks, smoke from smelters' fires, smells of freshly sawn timber, sounds of the hammering of brass and fleeting sights of elderly women dressed from head to toe in cream-coloured muslin. It all spells traditional North Africa – with a strong taste of Tunisia.

Slatit fjill   Radish and lemon salad

This is one of those perfect raw dishes in which the range of textures and flavours contrast and correspond brilliantly with each other. To make the radishes less sharp and more digestible, sprinkle the slices with salt and set them aside for an hour or so – the longer the better – so they release their juice, then rinse and drain. In Tunisian cuisine, it is considered more sophisticated to mince the radish finely, but the salad actually looks better with larger slices.

serves 4

12–15 firm, fat radishes, topped, tailed and thinly sliced
½ tbsp capers, drained and rinsed
1 tsp finely chopped preserved lemon (see page 187)
salt and ground black pepper, to taste
juice of ½ lemon
3 tbsp extra-virgin olive oil

1 - In a large bowl, mix together the radishes, capers and preserved lemon. Season to taste, then dress with the lemon juice and olive oil.

2 - Turn the salad thoroughly to coat evenly, and serve at room temperature.

Slatit houriya   Carrot and raisin salad

This simple salad is high in vitamins and makes an unusual starter as the sweet honey flavour comes through loud and clear. Dalila sometimes adds finely chopped tomatoes.

serves 2 (or 4 if served with another salad such as radish – see above)

500g (1lb 2oz) carrots, trimmed, peeled and grated
1 tbsp raisins
juice of ½ lemon
1 tbsp dark, runny honey
3 tbsp extra-virgin olive oil
salt and ground black pepper, to taste
2 tbsp finely chopped flat leaf parsley leaves, to garnish

1 - In a large bowl, combine the grated carrot with the raisins.

2 - In another bowl, mix together the lemon juice, honey, olive oil, salt and pepper, and stir into the carrot and raisin mixture to coat evenly. Garnish with the chopped parsley.

Slata mechouia
Grilled summer vegetable salad

This is a North African classic that can be eaten hot or cold. Its wonderful smoky flavour is obtained from grilling the vegetables over a *kanoun* – a small charcoal fire. The Western alternative would be to barbecue the vegetables, or to put them on a grid over a gas flame or, more conventionally, under an oven grill. The idea is to scorch the skins black, so be fearless with the temperature. The preparation of this dish is fiddly but more than worth the effort for the unusually flavoured and unctuous result.

serves 4

500g (1lb 2oz) tomatoes
1kg (2lb 4oz) green peppers
1 onion, skin left on
½ head garlic, cloves peeled and finely chopped
4–5 tbsp extra-virgin olive oil
2 tbsp lemon juice
1 tbsp *ras-el-hanout* (see page 187)
1 tbsp capers, drained and rinsed
2 tsp finely chopped preserved lemon (see page 187)
5 soft purple olives, pitted and sliced
salt, to taste

1 - Grill the tomatoes, peppers and onion for about 15 minutes, turning frequently, until scorched black all over.

2 - Scrape off most of the burnt skin. Halve, core and deseed the peppers. Rinse the peeled vegetables under running water and chop them into large chunks that are roughly the same size for each kind.

3 - In a large bowl, mix together the garlic, olive oil and lemon juice with the *ras-el-hanout*. Add the capers, preserved lemon and sliced olives. Add the chopped vegetables and turn them in the dressing to coat evenly. Add salt, to taste, then serve immediately.

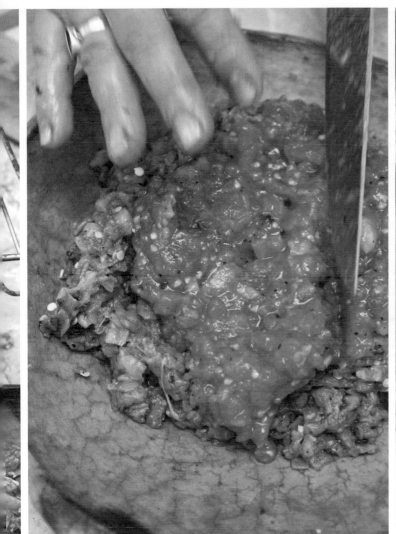

Doigts de Fatma   Fatma's fingers

This Tunisian version of Chinese spring rolls is named after the Muslim symbol for good luck: the hand of Fatma (Fatima), the daughter of Mohammed. Although time-consuming to make, the dish is one of Dalila's great favourites and rapidly devoured by house guests. The balance of textures is perfect: prawns, creamy ricotta and succulent capers.

serves 8–10 (about 30 fingers)

500g (1lb 2oz) shelled prawns, uncooked

leaves from ½ bunch of coriander, finely chopped

½ preserved lemon (see page 187), finely chopped

1 tbsp capers, drained and rinsed

1 heaped tsp *tabel* (see page 187)

1 tsp salt

½ tsp harissa (see page 186)

700g (1lb 9oz) ricotta cheese

1 egg, beaten

ground black pepper, to taste

30 rectangular sheets of 12 x 16cm (4½ x 6¼in) gossamer-thin filo pastry

vegetable oil, for frying

1 - Put the prawns in a bowl with the coriander, lemon, capers, spice, salt and harissa. Add the ricotta and mix together using your hands or a wooden spoon.

2 - Mix in the egg and pepper.

3 - Take a sheet of filo pastry, fold in half to strengthen, then dollop a tablespoon of the mixture in a line down the middle and form a roll, leaving the ends open.

4 - Pour enough vegetable oil to generously cover the bottom of a frying pan set over a medium heat, and heat it until it starts to smoke. Place the rolls carefully in the oil and fry for about 8–10 minutes until crisp and golden, turning over halfway through the cooking time.

5 - Remove the rolls from the oil with a slotted spoon, drain, then place on paper towels to absorb any excess oil. Serve warm or cold (but not too long after cooking). The rolls can be reheated in the oven if desired.

Purée de pommes de terre à la noix de muscade
Nutmeg mashed potatoes

Dalila's French-influenced specials continue with this side dish. There is a huge difference if the nutmeg is freshly grated and not a stale, old powder. This creamy mash makes an excellent accompaniment for simply prepared fish or meat.

serves 6

1kg (2lb 4oz) potatoes, peeled and cut into medium-sized chunks
pinch of salt
1 egg yolk
120ml (4fl oz) milk
freshly grated nutmeg, to taste
ground black pepper, to taste
3 tbsp single cream

1 - Boil the potatoes in a large pan of salted water over a medium heat until cooked through.

2 - Mash the potatoes thoroughly, add the egg yolk, milk, nutmeg and pepper, stirring well with each addition, then add the cream.

Lablabi   Spiced chickpea soup

Tunisians wax lyrical about this humble yet piquant soup that is sold on street corners as a cheap, nutritious snack. It is a great winter starter and is very easy to prepare. To make a richer soup, cook the chickpeas in chicken stock. Take care not to overdo the harissa.

serves 8

500g (1lb 2oz) dried chickpeas, soaked overnight in 2 litres (3½ pints) water
salt, to taste
½ tbsp harissa (see page 186)
2 tsp ground cumin (see page 186)
4–5 tbsp extra-virgin olive oil
5 large garlic cloves, peeled and crushed
squeeze of lemon juice (optional)
2 tbsp finely chopped coriander leaves (optional), to garnish

1 - Put the chickpeas in a large saucepan in their soaking water and bring to the boil over a medium heat. Boil vigorously for 10 minutes, reduce the heat and simmer for about 1½ hours, or until very soft, adding salt about 10 minutes before the end of the cooking time.

2 - Remove from the heat, then add the harissa, cumin, olive oil and garlic. Add a squeeze of lemon juice and the chopped coriander, if using, just before serving.

Seiches en leftiya Squid with turnip

This sounds like an unlikely combination, but it works! This dish is not supposed to be a stew, so although it should be juicy, be prepared to reduce the liquid. Serve with bulgur wheat, rice or couscous.

serves 6

1kg (2lb 4oz) squid, prepared, rinsed and cut
 ` into equal-sized parts
salt and ground black pepper, to taste
olive oil, for frying
1 large onion, peeled and roughly chopped
1 heaped tsp *ras-el-hanout* (see page 187)
1 heaped tsp turmeric

about 400ml (14fl oz) water
150g (5½oz) canned chickpeas,
 drained and rinsed
500g (1lb 2oz) small turnips, peeled
 and chopped into quarters
leaves from a bunch of flat leaf
 parsley, finely chopped

1 - Lightly season the squid with salt and pepper and set aside while preparing the other ingredients.
2 - Heat a little oil in a saucepan and add the onion, squid and spices. Cook over a low heat for a few minutes, stirring continuously, until the onion is soft. Add the water and chickpeas, stir well and bring to the boil. Lower the heat, cover with a lid and cook gently for about 45 minutes.
3 - Add the turnips and parsley, increase the heat and simmer hard for 15 minutes to reduce the liquid. Adjust the seasoning, if necessary, before serving.

Marquit ommalah   Pickle and meatball stew

This zingy, heart-warming meatball stew, one of Dalila's family favourites, is named after the pickles it contains. If you cannot find the pickles, try the recipe for Pickled Turnips on page 130 or replace them with a chopped preserved lemon (see page 187), seven or eight pickled onions and a tablespoon or two of capers. Whether or not you use the pickles, this dish is divinely nurturing and perfect for a winter evening. Serve with wholemeal bread to mop up the juices.

serves 8

1kg (2lb 4oz) minced beef

2 tsp *ras-el-hanout* (see page 187), plus 1 tsp more, or to taste

leaves from a bunch of fresh mint, finely chopped

salt and ground black pepper, to taste

about 250ml (9fl oz) water

3 tbsp olive oil

1 large onion, peeled and chopped

750g (1lb 10oz) tomatoes

½ tsp harissa (see page 186)

250–300g (9–10½oz) mixed pickles (carrots, turnips, celery)

4 red chilli peppers, left whole or chopped

8–10 green and black olives

1 - In a large bowl, mix together the minced beef, 2 tsp *ras-el-hanout*, mint, seasoning and enough of the water to make a moist, kneadable mixture. Form into small balls (about 3cm/1¼in in diameter) or little sausages.

2 - Heat the olive oil in a frying pan, add the onion and fry gently until soft.

3 - Make a cross at the base of all but one of the tomatoes and plunge these into boiling water for 30 seconds. Transfer to cold water. Drain and remove the loosened skins. Cut out the cores, then chop and add to the sizzling onion. Stir the mixture over a medium heat for a few minutes then cover and simmer hard so that the tomatoes release their juices and a sauce is created.

4 - Add the meatballs or sausages to the sauce, then the harissa and 1 tsp more of *ras-el-hanout*, or to taste.

5 - Rinse the pickles under running water, add to the mix and simmer gently for a further 40 minutes.

6 - Just before serving, add the chilli peppers, olives and remaining tomato, chopped, for visual panache. Adjust the salt, if necessary, then serve in a large, wide bowl.

Marquit jilbana   Lamb, artichoke and pea stew

The peas dominate the flavour of this stew, and their sheer quantity also monopolize its appearance, with the yellow saffron kicking in behind. If necessary, you can replace the fresh artichoke hearts and peas with canned/bottled or frozen versions. Dalila always smiles when this dish is mentioned and Ahmed seems only too happy to shell mountains of fresh peas in anticipation of the meal to come. It's a real family dish and perfect on a cool spring or summer evening.

serves 4

> 175ml (6fl oz) olive oil
> 750g (1lb 10oz) boned leg of lamb, cut into large chunks
> 2 onions, peeled and finely chopped
> 1 tsp saffron, crumbled
> salt and ground black pepper, to taste
> about 1 litre (1¾ pint) water
> 750g (1lb 10oz) shelled peas, fresh or frozen
> leaves from a bunch of flat leaf parsley, roughly chopped
> 1 lemon, sliced and pips removed
> 6 cooked artichoke hearts, fresh or canned/bottled, quartered

1 - Heat the olive oil in a deep saucepan, then add the lamb, onion, saffron, salt and pepper. Cook over a medium heat, stirring continuously, for about 10 minutes, or until the onion is soft.

2 - Add enough water to submerge the ingredients, cover the saucepan and simmer gently for about 40–50 minutes, or until the lamb is cooked through, stirring and checking the water level occasionally.

3 - Add the peas, parsley, lemon slices and more water, if necessary, and simmer for a further 10 minutes.

4 - Add the artichoke hearts and continue to cook on a low heat for a further 5–10 minutes. Remove the lemon slices before serving.

Daurade à l'ail   Sea bream with garlic

This dish originated with Dalila's French employers and is a firm favourite during the hot days of spring and summer. Although it sounds as if you will be breathing garlic fire for days, this is not the case, as the garlic merely gives a mild flavour to the fish – no more. The dish looks good, is light on the stomach and quick to prepare.

serves 4–5

2 large sea bream, scaled, gutted and cleaned
6 large garlic cloves, peeled and roughly chopped
1 large tomato, sliced
1 lemon, sliced
salt and ground black pepper, to taste
bunch of coriander, roughly chopped
olive oil, to drizzle

1 - Preheat the oven to 200°C/400°F/Gas mark 6. Place the fish on a lightly oiled oven dish and stuff with the garlic cloves.

2 - Arrange the tomato and lemon slices over the fish, then sprinkle with salt, pepper and coriander. Drizzle generously with the olive oil.

3 - Cover the fish in kitchen foil and bake in the preheated oven for 20–25 minutes, depending on the size of the fish, until cooked through.

Samsa   Almond and sesame pastries

These delectable pastries can be served warm or cold. Originally introduced by the Ottoman Turks and now a Tunisian classic, *samsa* are usually served with mint tea to finish off a meal. Women often make them together, chatting as they roll up the pastry envelopes.

serves 10 (makes about 30 pastries)

250g (9oz) icing sugar
250g (9oz) ground almonds
200g (7oz) ground sesame seeds
2 tbsp finely grated orange zest (optional)
4–5 tbsp rose water
2 egg whites
about 30 sheets of 25 x 10cm (10 x 4in) gossamer-thin filo pastry
vegetable oil, for deep-frying
handful of blanched almonds, chopped, to decorate

syrup:
500ml (18fl oz) water
250g (9oz) caster sugar
juice of ½ lemon
1 tbsp geranium or orange-blossom water

1 - Put the icing sugar, almonds, sesame seeds and orange zest (if using) in a bowl. Add the rose water and 1 egg white and knead the mixture together to form a stiff paste.

2 - Take a rectangle of pastry, place ½ tbsp of the mixture at one end, then fold to the left, then to the right, continuing in the same way to the end of the strip. This creates a triangular envelope. Tuck in the ends and seal with a little egg white. Alternatively (and more easily) make a cigar-shaped roll, folding in the ends as you go.

3 - Heat about 2cm (¾in) of vegetable oil in a frying pan set over a medium heat, until the oil starts to smoke. Reduce the heat. Lower the parcels – one by one or two at a time – into the oil, turning a couple of times and scooping hot oil over the top. Remove with a slotted spoon after 2–3 minutes. Place them on paper towels to absorb any excess oil, then put aside in a colander.

4 - To make the syrup, heat the water in a saucepan set over a high heat. When it boils, add the sugar, reduce to a low heat and stir for about 10 minutes until the sugar has dissolved. Add the lemon juice and simmer gently until a syrup is formed. Remove from the heat and add the geranium or orange-blossom water.

5 - Using a slotted spoon, dip each pastry in the syrup for a couple of seconds, remove and return to the colander. Arrange the *samsa* on a serving plate and decorate with chopped almonds.

Slatit bordgane   Orange and mint salad

Oranges are not the only fruit in North Africa, but at certain times of the year it can seem that way.
The most intoxicating moment comes in April, when the orange blossom is in full bloom and the
heady perfume wafts through the patios of the medina. To capture a sense of this, try making this
dessert. Light, fragrant and refreshing, it is a perfect conclusion to one of Dalila's meals.

serves 4

6 blood oranges, peeled, pith removed
2–3 tsp orange-blossom water
2 tbsp orange peel, cut into fine matchsticks
3 tbsp caster sugar
150ml (5fl oz) water
leaves from a bunch of fresh mint, finely shredded
100g (3½oz) blanched almonds, sliced, to decorate

1 - Slice the peeled oranges thinly, removing any pips. Arrange in a glass bowl and sprinkle with
the orange-blossom water.

2 - In a small saucepan, mix together the remaining ingredients and simmer over a low heat for
15 minutes.

3 - Pour the sauce over the oranges and decorate with the almonds.

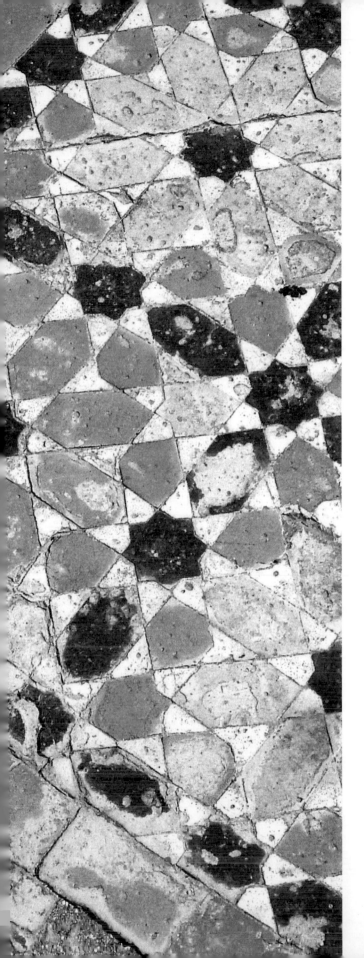

CARTHAGE

قرطاج

Mina Ben-Miled

'SHE'S ONE OF THE FEW HOSTESSES WHO REALLY KNOWS HER TRADITIONAL CUISINE AND YET IS ABLE TO TRANSFORM IT IN A BALANCED WAY.'

Down a palm-lined avenue within spitting distance of the 3,000-year-old ruins of Queen Dido's palace, and with the ultramarine Mediterranean as a backdrop, stands a large, comfortable 1960s villa. The white, neo-modernist style would not look out of place in Miami; Carthage is the smartest of the so-called northern suburbs of Tunis. Inside, contemporary artwork, Tunisian handicrafts, French art books and modern furniture contribute to a unique tone created by its owners, the interior designer Mina Ben-Miled and her architect husband. This dauntingly dynamic, chic woman in her 40s manages to juggle her business with trips abroad, intellectual interests and a string of dinner parties, all accomplished in an atmosphere of measured mayhem.

A lunch or dinner party at Mina's is legendary among the intelligentsia of Tunis and will take place either inside, around an elegant circular dining table, or on a poolside terrace in a verdant garden strewn with Roman and Punic fragments. Mina is the first to admit that she could not manage all this entertaining without the live-in help, Sabiha, a shy, pretty young Tunisian from Sousse who has worked in the kitchen beside her for over five years. Together they operate a tight ship, notwithstanding some animated arguments, usually concerning a fine gastronomic point: a sure sign that they know each other – and their food – very well.

'I married young,' explains Mina, 'so I never really learned cooking at home, like most Tunisian women. Neither my mother nor my grandmother were typical as they both worked full time in education and weren't stay-at-home housewives. But my grandmother was an excellent cook as she nurtured my grandfather, who was a writer before he became Minister of Education after Independence. My mother started cooking later in life and, thank goodness, greatly improved! They both gave me a taste for lighter, less oily food than is usually the case in Tunisia.' While talking, Mina is checking on a *chakchouka* (Tunisian ratatouille) bubbling on the stove. Unscrewing a recycled whisky bottle, she pours in a trickle of thick, mossy-green olive oil. 'This comes from my parents' farm in Cap Bon, the area where I grew up,' she says. 'It's exquisite. I've been using it for years and nothing else will do!'

In the relatively small kitchen ('It's still awaiting a makeover!'), Mina darts around while Sabiha works silently and steadfastly, rapidly chopping, stirring and pulling out extra ingredients from a row of jam jars filled with spices. The secret of their success lies in the combination of Sabiha's intuitive sense of traditional ingredients and methods and Mina's evolved global tastes and ideas. Tradition meets innovation, with each holding the other in check.

Social life in the northern suburbs is hectic, and Mina's reputation for impromptu or more formal spreads is well established. 'She's one of the few hostesses who really knows her traditional cuisine and yet is able to transform it in a balanced way,' comments a friend. Mina explains how she composes a meal. 'When I make a buffet dinner I ensure every dish goes together, even if my guests do not taste them all at once,' she says. 'What I make depends entirely on the season and who's coming to dinner. If it's Ramadan, for example, I only make traditional dishes, while for my regular circle of friends I'll prepare something Mediterranean and usually quite light, very often with fish as a main course. I only ever serve one dessert, maybe slices of fresh melon or a sorbet, followed by mint tea and patisseries. Everyone is so health- and waistline-conscious these days – including me!' she groans. 'The only problem with entertaining is remembering what I cooked for guests the previous time. And sometimes a friend will mention a special dish they ate at my house – and I'm perplexed!' It's lucky Mina can confess to such absent-mindedness, or otherwise she really would be the superwoman of Carthage.

Despite Mina's attention to detail, she does not waste time on labour-intensive preparations of fresh ingredients unless they are absolutely essential to the flavour. If there is a more efficient, shorter

route, she will follow it. Frozen food occasionally comes into play, whether home-prepared or a packet straight from the supermarket freezer. 'Now that my children have left home we eat a lot less meat,' she says. 'If it's just my husband and myself in the evening, we often just have soup and salad or pasta,' she says. 'And we rarely make couscous these days – it is too much both in terms of preparation and to eat, but, yes, it is a pillar of Tunisian cuisine.'

Most of the produce comes from the select food market of La Marsa, a 10-minute drive from home and close to her design shop and office. Here Mina stocks up on meat, fresh fish, spices, olives, pickles and fantastically glossy fruit and vegetables, all in a relatively quick turnaround. Her decisive, communicative manner means she knows the stallholders and their produce as well as they know her. Well acquainted with her tastes, they will sometimes put aside a favourite cut of meat or fish for her.

Mina, the voice of innovation, fishes out her mobile ringing at the bottom of a large handbag, rattles off instructions to her assistant in Arabic sprinkled with French, then leaps up to go. 'My husband says I exhaust him!' she laughs as she disappears out the door trailing a pashmina shawl. Cooking is clearly only one aspect of her daily life, but its quality is no less for it.

CARTHAGE

It takes barely half an hour from central Tunis to reach the seaside suburbs that flounce along the Bay of Tunis. A Roman causeway takes you across a vast lagoon to reach the desirable *banlieue nord* (northern suburbs): La Goulette, Sidi Bou Said and La Marsa, as well as Carthage. Oddly, this area rather than the medina was the centre of ancient food history, with Carthage as the erstwhile capital of the Mediterranean's first great trading empire. This dates back to Dido, the legendary Phoenician queen who chose a tragic end: having been abandoned by her lover Aeneas, she plunged into the flames of a pyre on Carthage beach. Seven hundred years later, the town itself was razed to the ground by the Romans.

The Carthaginian approach to food and agriculture was longer-lasting. From the 6th century BC, they developed ingenious techniques to cultivate fruit, nuts, grains, grapes, dates and olives on a massive scale. Carthaginian olive oil became highly sought after and rivalled that of Greece, while the wine was quaffed from Rome to Etrusca and Greece. Sadly, few direct written records of their successful techniques remain as these were devoured by the flames of Carthage's downfall. Among them was a magnum opus by Magon, the greatest agronomist of antiquity. This 28-volume treatise was so influential that both the Greeks and the Romans consulted it, translating salient sections and thus preserving a few choice titbits. A prime example is Magon's advice on choosing oxen: 'They must be young, stocky and sturdy of limb with long horns, darkish and healthy, a wide and wrinkled forehead, hairy ears and black eyes and chops, the nostrils well opened and turned back, the neck long and muscular, the dewlap full and descending to the knees, the chest well developed, broad shoulders, the belly big like that of a cow in calf, the flanks long, the loins broad, the back straight and flat or a little depressed in the middle, the buttocks rounded, the legs thick and straight, rather short than long, the knees straight, the hooves large, the tail long and hairy...' With requirements as stringent as these, no wonder the Carthaginians had such an empire.

Today, the elegant seaside villas of Carthage belong to Tunisian professionals, foreign ambassadors, and the President, an occasional occupant, whose hilltop palace commands the best views. Close by, wedged between cypress trees and cacti, are crumbling pieces of the past, from the mysterious Phoenician children's cemetery of Tophet, to Roman baths and the ruined villas of the Classical world.

Contemporary food lovers descend on Carthage's offshoot, La Goulette (see pages 142–161), where two parallel avenues offer wall-to-wall fish restaurants and cafés. On a balmy evening, every table will be occupied by a Tunisian couple or family. Fish is prolific in these waters, inspiring amateur fishermen to bob around in dinghies while professionals land dozens of squid pots. Out of season, when the beaches have emptied and the restaurants see only a handful of customers, there is a stronger sense of what has long gone. But what does not change – today as in Queen Dido's time – is the dazzlingly clear light of the Mediterranean.

Chakchouka tmatim wa filfil   Tunisian ratatouille

Chakchouka is excellent as a summer side dish or starter to be eaten hot or cold. Mina stresses the importance of not overcooking the pepper, as it is this that gives the dish its character.

serves 4

2 tbsp olive oil
2 small onions, peeled and finely chopped
500g (1lb 2oz) tomatoes, chopped
1 tbsp *tabel* (see page 187)
½ tsp caraway seeds
1 tsp harissa (optional – see page 186)
6 garlic cloves, peeled and crushed
ground black pepper, to taste
250g (9oz) green pepper, cored, deseeded and chopped
salt, to taste

1 - Heat the oil in a frying pan and fry the onion for a few minutes over a medium heat, then add the tomatoes, spices and harissa. Increase the heat and simmer hard to reduce. Add the garlic and black pepper.

2 - Lower the heat, cover and simmer gently for about 10 minutes.

3 - Add the peppers and salt. Cover and cook for a further 10–15 minutes. Serve warm.

Torshi   Pickled turnips

Pickles, usually a mixture of turnips, carrots and celery, are typical in Tunisian cooking and are often added to couscous for extra bite. They are easy to make (though they need to be prepared at least 3 hours in advance) and keep well in the refrigerator for several months, unopened. Mina serves them in small bowls alongside olives with an aperitif. If you like fiery flavours, add half a teaspoon of harissa diluted in a little water. The citrus juice can be replaced by vinegar, if desired.

serves 4

500g (1lb 2oz) small, young turnips, trimmed, peeled and finely sliced
salt, to taste
juice of 1 lemon
juice of 1 Seville orange
handful of aniseed or caraway seeds

1 - Sprinkle the turnip generously with salt and put aside for 1 hour so it releases its juices.

2 - Squeeze the lemon and orange juice over the turnip and sprinkle with aniseed or caraway seeds. Put into a sterilized glass jar and seal to make airtight.

Shorbat frik   Barley and lamb soup

This highly nutritious soup has a wonderful velvety texture thanks to the slow cooking and the consistency of the barley. Mina likes it so well cooked that the barley has almost melted into the juices. As there is relatively little meat, try to use lamb's neck, which is full of flavour.

serves 6–8

vegetable oil, for frying
1 onion, peeled and finely chopped
200g (7oz) cracked barley
400g (14oz) lamb's neck or shoulder, cut into large chunks
2–3 sticks celery, including leaves, thinly sliced
6 tbsp finely chopped flat leaf parsley leaves
6 garlic cloves, peeled and crushed
50g (1¾oz) dried chickpeas, soaked overnight, drained and rinsed
2 tbsp tomato purée
3 tbsp frozen peas
1½ litres (2¾ pints) water
salt, to taste
juice of 1 large lemon (optional)
fresh coriander leaves, chopped, to garnish (optional)

1 - In a large saucepan, heat a little vegetable oil and fry the onion over a medium heat until golden, then add the barley. Cook, stirring continuously, for 5 minutes then add the lamb, celery and parsley.

2 - Add the garlic, chickpeas, tomato purée, peas and half the water. Simmer for a further 10 minutes then add the remaining water plus salt to taste.

3 - Cover the pan, reduce to a low heat and simmer very gently for about 2 hours.

4 - For an extra kick, squeeze some lemon juice into the soup just before serving and garnish with chopped coriander.

Salade romaine   Orange, cos and feta salad

Tunisia's original salad ingredient was Cos lettuce (*salade romaine*), as no other kinds were cultivated there. The firm leaves are perfect in this sweet and salty summer salad.

serves 4–6

1 tbsp red wine vinegar
3 tbsp extra-virgin olive oil
salt and ground black pepper, to taste
1 large Cos lettuce, leaves separated
100g (3½oz) feta cheese, cubed
1 orange, peeled, pith removed, and chopped
juice of 1 orange

1 - Combine the vinegar, olive oil, salt and pepper in a bowl to make a vinaigrette, then set aside.
2 - Slice the lettuce finely across the leaves to make strips, put in a salad bowl with the feta and orange, and sprinkle with the orange juice.
3 - Pour the vinaigrette over the salad just before serving, and turn to cover evenly.

Slata tounsiya but tiffah   Tunisian salad

Tunisia's ubiquitous national salad is refreshing, colourful and oil-free. It makes a perfect summer starter with a minty hit. The apple rings the changes and you could also add capers and finely chopped preserved lemon (see page 187). Do not make it too far in advance or it will lose its crispness.

serves 6–8

4 small cucumbers, peeled and diced
1 small red onion, peeled and diced
3 tomatoes, diced
3 green peppers, cored, deseeded and diced
2 apples (an acidic variety such as Cox), peeled, cored and chopped
juice of 1 lemon
1 tbsp dried mint (see page 186)
salt, to taste

to garnish:
handful of small black olives
handful of fresh mint leaves

1 - Mix together all the chopped vegetables and apples in a large salad bowl, add the lemon juice and sprinkle with dried mint. Season with salt.
2 - Dress with olives and fresh mint leaves and serve immediately.

Tajine sebnakh   Baked spinach tagine

Tunisian tagines are nothing like Moroccan ones; instead they are somewhere between an omelette and a quiche and always baked in the oven. This quite complex and very filling dish looks deceptively like a fat spinach tortilla. In fact it contains a multitude of flavours. Mina likes plenty of ricotta to add to the unctuousness – but this shouldn't mask the other flavours, and can even be left out.

serves 6–8

2 onions, peeled and chopped

vegetable oil, for frying and for oiling dish

2–3 garlic cloves, peeled (optional)

500g (1lb 2oz) chicken thighs (on the bone, skin left on)

175ml (6fl oz) water

3 cooked artichoke hearts, fresh or canned/bottled, chopped

150–200g (5½–7oz) frozen peas

1kg (2lb 4oz) spinach, stalks removed

100g (3½oz) hard cheese, such as Gruyère, grated

5–6 eggs, beaten

1 tsp turmeric

ground black pepper, to taste

1 tsp grated nutmeg

salt, to taste

flour, to dust dish

200g (7oz) ricotta cheese (optional), drained and sliced

1 - In a large frying pan, gently fry the onion in a little vegetable oil for a few minutes. Add the garlic (if using) and chicken thighs and continue frying for about 10 minutes.

2 - Stir in the water, cover, and simmer gently over a low heat for about 20 minutes. Add the artichoke hearts and cook for a further 10 minutes.

3 - Preheat the oven to 200°C/400°F/Gas mark 6. Part-cook the peas for a few minutes in some boiling water in a separate saucepan, then drain and add to the main mixture.

4 - Place the spinach in a bowl, cover with boiling water, stir quickly then drain in a colander, but keep back 3–4 tbsp water and add this to the chicken.

5 - When the chicken is cooked through, remove the skin from each thigh, then remove the meat from the bone and shred into pieces. Mix the chicken with the spinach, then add the hard cheese, eggs, turmeric, pepper and nutmeg. Add salt to taste.

6 - Lightly coat a round oven dish (about 30cm/12in in diameter) with vegetable oil and sprinkle with a little flour. Fill with most of the chicken mixture then cover with sliced ricotta, if desired, finishing with a final layer of the chicken mixture.

7 - Bake low down in the preheated oven for about 25 minutes, or until set. Serve immediately, turned out onto a large, flat dish.

Poisson à la kerkennaise   Fish in tomato and garlic sauce

This is an easy but striking main course with a wonderful array of flavours. Its success depends on the freshness of the fish, so only choose those with really sparkling eyes and firm glossy scales.

serves 8

750g (1lb 10oz) tomatoes
4–5 tbsp olive oil
5 garlic cloves, peeled and crushed
2 large fish such as sea bream (about 1½kg/3lb 5oz), scaled, gutted and cleaned
salt and ground black pepper, to taste
juice of 1 lemon

to garnish:
½ preserved lemon (see page 187), finely chopped
1 green pepper, cored, deseeded and diced

1 - Preheat the oven to 220°C/425°F/Gas mark 7.

2 - Make a cross at the base of each tomato and plunge them into boiling water for 30 seconds. Transfer to cold water. Drain and remove the loosened skins. Cut the flesh into chunks.

3 - Heat 2 tbsp olive oil in a saucepan over a low heat and add the tomatoes. Add the garlic, cover and simmer for about 30 minutes to make a sauce.

4 - Meanwhile, sprinkle the inside of each fish with salt and pepper then lay on an oiled ovenproof dish. Drizzle each fish generously with the remaining olive oil and the lemon juice.

5 - Bake the fish in the preheated oven for 5 minutes, then turn the heat down to 190°C/375°F/ Gas mark 5 and bake for a further 25–30 minutes, until cooked through. Remove the fish from the oven, put onto a serving dish and cover with the tomato and garlic sauce. Garnish with the preserved lemon and green pepper.

Tajine malsouka   Baked chicken and pastry tagine

This extremely refined dish of Turkish origin is never found in restaurants as it is far too complex.
It is a great party piece, a kind of magician's trump card, and very close to a Moroccan pastilla in
form (see page 93), though without the sweetness. It looks like a pie but conceals an interior that
alternates crunch with creaminess plus a strong saffron hit. The chicken can be replaced by minced
beef or chopped veal. If made in advance, which may be advisable, reheat in a medium oven for
5 minutes. Serve it warm on a completely flat dish or, as Mina does, on a cake stand – with a flourish.

serves 6–8

  3 onions, peeled and chopped
  vegetable oil, for frying and brushing the pastry and dish
  1kg (2lb 4oz) chicken thighs (on the bone, skin left on)
  1–2 tsp crushed saffron threads, or freshly ground nutmeg, mixed with a little water
  100g (3½oz) hard cheese, such as Gruyère, grated
  4 eggs, beaten
  salt and ground black pepper, to taste
  12 large rounds filo pastry, each about 25–30cm (10–12in) in diameter
  250g (9oz) ricotta cheese, thinly sliced
  2 egg yolks mixed with 1–2 tsp vegetable oil, to glaze

1 - In a frying pan, fry the onion in a little vegetable oil for a few minutes, until soft. Add the chicken and 200–250ml (7–9fl oz) water, cover, then cook for 45 minutes, or until the chicken is cooked through, turning from time to time. Preheat the oven to 190°C/375°F/Gas mark 5.

2 - Discard the chicken skin, remove the meat from the bone and place the pieces in a bowl.

3 - Pour the saffron or ground nutmeg paste over the chicken, then stir in the grated cheese and 2–3 tbsp of water to make an unctuous mixture. Stir in the beaten eggs and season.

4 - Oil an ovenproof pie or quiche dish about the same size as the rounds of filo pastry. Overlap five rounds of the filo pastry inside, lightly brushing each sheet with vegetable oil as you go, and allowing at least a third to hang over the edge of the dish. Place a final, sixth piece of pastry in the centre to reinforce the base.

5 - Pour in most of the chicken mixture, followed by a layer of sliced ricotta then a final layer of the chicken. Fold the overhanging filo pastry lightly over the top so that it is just 'wrapped' but not tightly. Stick the edges together using a pastry brush and the glaze. Place another layer of filo on the top, tucking the edges into the side of the dish, then four more pieces of filo, brushing them with the glaze as you go. Finish with more glaze brushed on top.

6 - Place the tagine low down in the oven for about 20–25 minutes. The pastry will be crisp and golden when the dish is ready. Serve hot, turned out onto a flat dish and cut like a cake.

Borghol   Baked bulgur wheat

This is a legacy from the Ottomans as bulgur wheat is not indigenous to North Africa. The dry, slightly crunchy consistency infused with olive oil and spices is so much better than that of boiled bulgur wheat, which often ends up soggy. For extra freshness, toss in some diced tomatoes with the peas.

serves 6

500g (1lb 2oz) bulgur wheat
2–3 onions, peeled and finely chopped
5–6 large garlic cloves, peeled and crushed
1 heaped tbsp *tabel* (see page 187)
salt and ground black pepper, to taste
4–5 tbsp olive oil
125g (4½oz) cooked peas

1 - Preheat the oven to 190°C/375°F/Gas mark 5. Put the bulgur wheat, onion, garlic, *tabel* and salt and pepper into an ovenproof dish with a lid. Stir in enough olive oil to coat the grains of bulgur wheat, then pour in sufficient water to cover. Cover and bake in the oven for 50 minutes.

2 - Remove the dish from the oven and stir in the cooked peas before serving.

Gâteau aux pistaches   Pistachio cake

This dessert looks solid but slips down easily after a substantial main course. The traditional, far richer and heavier version uses dried fruit, butter and sugar and the cake is coated in syrup.

serves 8

350g (12oz) shelled pistachios
8–9 egg whites
pinch of salt
250g (9oz) caster sugar

1 - Preheat the oven to 110°C/225°F/Gas mark ¼. Roast the pistachios for 10–15 minutes. Leave to cool before removing the skins by rubbing them off in a clean tea towel. Cool completely then grind coarsely in a food processor. Turn the oven up to 200°C/400°F/Gas mark 6.

2 - Put the egg whites in a clean bowl. Add the salt and whisk until they stand up in peaks, then slowly add the sugar and fold in the ground pistachios, keeping back a handful to decorate.

3 - Grease an ovenproof quiche dish and gently fill with the mixture, being careful not to break up the foam.

4 - Put the dish in a large bowl or baking tin of water, and place in the oven for about 25 minutes. The cake should rise like a soufflé. Serve at room temperature.

Citronnade Lemon squash

The history of citrus fruit in North Africa is very hazy, but it is thought that Egyptians were the first to create lemonade in around AD 1,000. This classic squash is ideal for a hot summer's day. What makes it memorable is the sharp tang of the lemon skin. Adjust the amount of sugar according to your taste. Fresh mint adds an extra kick.

serves 8

750g (1lb 10oz) unwaxed lemons, quartered
3 litres (5¼ pints) water
300g (10½oz) caster sugar, or to taste
ice cubes, to serve
fresh mint sprigs, to decorate

1 - Place the lemons in a large saucepan with 1 litre (1¾ pints) of the water and bring to the boil. Reduce the heat and simmer, covered, for about 30 minutes.

2 - Take the saucepan off the heat and pulverize the lemons with a blending stick or in a liquidizer until the mixture foams and the lemons are completely broken up into a pulp.

3 - Stir in the remaining 2 litres (3½ pints) of water and pour the mixture through a sieve, pushing down on the pulp with the back of a spoon to extract the maximum flavour.

4 - Pour the sugar into the juice and stir well, then allow to cool and chill in the refrigerator.

5 - Serve the squash in a large glass jug with ice cubes. Decorate with fresh mint sprigs.

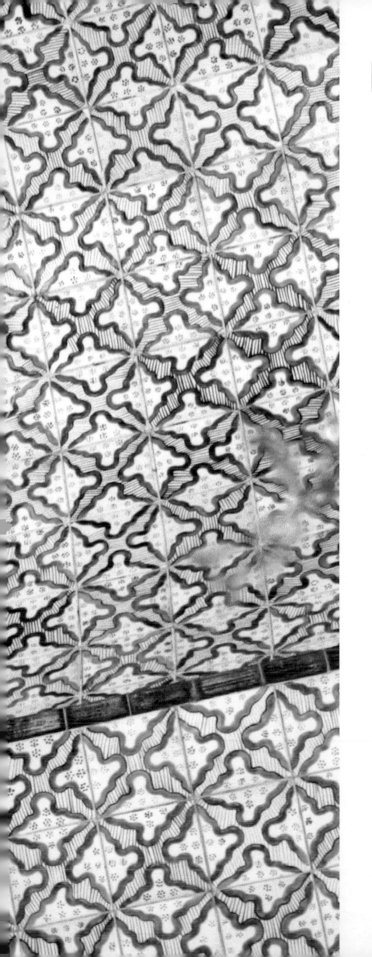

LA GOULETTE

حلق الوادي

Jacob Lellouche

'WE LIKE TO KEEP THE REAL FLAVOUR OF EACH ELEMENT, SO USE FEW SPICES AND HERBS.'

Just outside Tunis is La Goulette (literally the 'gullet'), a sleepy seaside resort of whitewashed villas. Those in the know turn off the main avenue, down a side street and enter the gates of a delightfully ramshackle house standing in an oasis of loquat trees, scarlet hibiscus and palm trees. It looks as intriguing as its discreet sign, 'Mama Lilie'. What lies within is a *table d'hôte* specializing in Tunisian-Jewish home cooking.

In the large white kitchen is the eponymous Lilie, an 80-year-old blonde with big gold earrings, sitting squarely on a stool and shelling peas into a bucket. Soon she turns to calmly rolling fish balls between the palms of her hands. Beside the stove stands her 43-year-old son, Jacob Lellouche, tall, fit and extravagantly mustachioed, and the brain behind the cuisine. Between the two of them and one helper, they feed three or four tables of aficionados six days a week. Most are Tunisian Jews nostalgic for traditional fare, and many have become friends. As a result, the atmosphere is more like an informal lunch or dinner party than a restaurant, with Jacob and Lilie sitting down to chat in a homely dining room plastered with family mementoes. 'Some clients borrow books or CDs, and sometimes I even forget to charge them!' jokes Jacob.

Jacob's approach to food is cerebral, in contrast to Lilie's more intuitive style. But he nonetheless openly admits that, in classic Jewish mode, the influence of his mother has been primordial. 'I started cooking out of necessity when I was a student in Paris,' he relates. 'I didn't have that much money but had no desire to eat the usual *steak-frites* or sandwiches, so I would phone her for recipes. What I missed above all was her couscous – and that's how my passion for food really started.'

With the mass exodus of Jews from Tunisia in the 1940s (only 1,400 remain of what was once a population of 400,000), many of the survivors have forgotten the origins of their cuisine, and this is what Jacob is reviving, with a contemporary twist. The kitchen looks surprisingly bare other than the fresh ingredients piled up on one long, central table which is the centre of activities. The absence of spices and condiments turns out to reflect Jacob's philosophy of letting the basic ingredients speak for themselves. 'We like to keep the real flavour of each element, so use few spices and herbs. My main input has been to make dishes lighter, less oily – I'm very aware of nutrition. And, although we are the only kosher eating place left in Tunis, it's not a living museum, I don't want to be stuck.' After a moment of thought, he adds: 'But before innovation you need to know your own traditions.'

Every morning, Jacob orchestrates events, from deliveries to preparing tables or chivvying his mother along. Most of the shopping is done locally at the covered market but the meat has to come from a kosher butcher. 'It's a problem finding kosher ingredients,' he explains, 'so I have one or two sent from Paris, for example soya cream, which I use for desserts. That's because we observe *kashrut*, the Jewish dietary laws which forbid eating dairy products after meat.'

Jacob is pleased with the mellow lifestyle of La Goulette. 'I'm very attached to it. Fifteen generations of my family were born here, going back to the Ottomans in the 16th century. Originally, though, we were from Spain – true Sephardim. My surname, Lellouche, comes from 'Al Alouch', meaning shepherd, so what I do now vaguely follows the family tradition I suppose – it's still about food!'

As we talk, Jacob prepares the various elements which make up his *kémia*, the *amuse-gueules* which are automatically served with an aperitif. His visual sense is reflected as much in the arrangement of dishes as in his other occupation – designing hand-painted wooden handicrafts in a studio across the road. 'The visual side of cooking developed when I was working in advertising in Paris,' he relates. 'There was a lot of entertaining to do and my guests were typically Parisian and very discerning.'

Jacob also talks eloquently about the history of Jewish-Tunisian cuisine. 'It's a patchwork from Spain, Italy, Greece, Turkey, Egypt and France, and an incredibly rich and varied Mediterranean journey,' he explains. 'I think Jews have a kind of gastronomic memory – a bit Proustian – which means we link certain tastes to specific occasions. And we Tunisian Jews have more celebrations than Algerian or Moroccan Jews – so it's logical that there are more dishes we're passionate about!

'It was only when I was 25, after years of practice, that my mother finally admitted that my couscous was as good as hers. That was a big day for me! Since then I've experimented with dozens of dishes, here and also in Paris, whenever I return to see my children. I feel cooking is the high point of communication as it combines all the senses at once – even sound. Think of the sizzling of an onion – it's like a kind of music...' His mind spirals silently away.

After lunch, as the languid tones of Sara Montiel crackle on what sounds like an ageing gramophone, Lilie abandons the mini-dramas of the kitchen. She's a local star, that's obvious from the way she dresses and her demeanour, and she talks passionately about cooking. 'As there were ten children in my family, the food was never fantastic,' she recalls. 'In fact my fiancé refused to eat at my home because he found it so unappetizing! So he took me off to watch and learn with his mother who was a brilliant cook, a natural Cordon Bleu. It meant that I had to meet high standards right from the start. Nowadays I don't even need to taste what I cook – it's automatic and I can judge visually.'

Mother and son have an easy-going relationship full of mutual admiration. 'I have great confidence in Jacob,' says Lilie. 'He really knows how to cook and has always been very picky. Both he and his father were so demanding that I sometimes had to make two different soups – one with beans and the other with chickpeas!' At this she takes off her apron, adjusts her lipstick and sweeps off for her siesta.

'A real Jewish mother,' sighs Jacob.

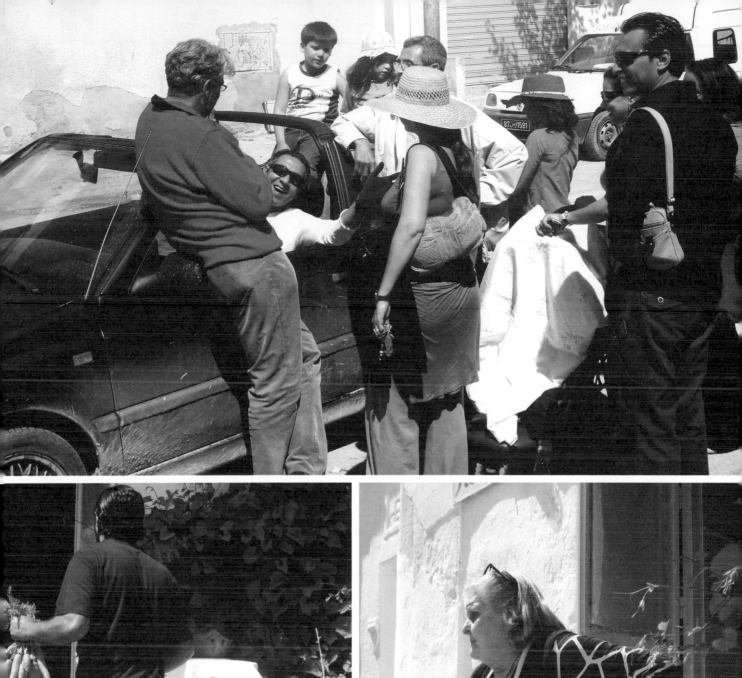

KEMIA   MIXED APPETIZERS

This Tunisian version of mezze is typical of Jewish-Tunisian tables. The little saucers of vegetables and pickles accompany Boukha, a dry liqueur made from fermented and distilled prickly pears (*figues de Barbarie*), and not from figs, as is so often said. It is drunk chilled, like vodka shots.

serves 4–6

Batata bel kamoun   Spicy potato salad

200g (7oz) potatoes, peeled and chopped into halves or quarters
salt, to taste

dressing:
2 tbsp extra-virgin olive oil
1 tbsp lemon juice
1 tsp harissa (see page 186)
1 tsp ground cumin (see page 186)
salt, to taste

1 - Boil the potatoes in a saucepan of salted water until cooked, then dice.

2 - Mix together the olive oil and lemon juice, then add the harissa, cumin and salt.

3 - Turn the potatoes in the dressing to coat evenly.

Torchi chfenaria   Carrot and caraway salad

200g (7oz) carrots, trimmed, peeled and cut into thick rounds
salt, to taste

dressing:
2 tbsp extra-virgin olive oil
1 tbsp lemon juice
1 tsp harissa (see page 186)
1 tsp caraway seeds
salt, to taste

1 - Boil the carrots in a saucepan of salted water until cooked.

2 - Mix together the olive oil and lemon juice and then add the harissa, caraway seeds and salt.

3 - Turn the carrots in the dressing to coat evenly.

Slatit badhinjan   Aubergine salad

olive oil, for frying
1 onion, peeled and thinly sliced
2 aubergines, trimmed and diced
1 tbsp capers, drained and rinsed

dressing:
3 tbsp extra-virgin olive oil
1 tbsp red wine vinegar
1 tsp harissa (see page 186)
½ tsp ground coriander
½ tsp caraway seeds
salt, to taste

1 - Heat a little oil in a frying pan and lightly fry the onion. Remove from the pan.

2 - Add a little more oil to the frying pan and fry the diced aubergines until lightly browned and cooked through. Add the onion and capers.

3 - Mix together the olive oil and vinegar, then add the harissa, coriander, caraway seeds and salt.

4 - Toss the vegetables and capers in the dressing to coat evenly.

Torchi khel   Fresh pickled vegetables

2 carrots, peeled
2 small turnips, peeled
2 courgettes, trimmed
1 green pepper, cored and deseeded
2 sticks celery
half a head of fennel, trimmed
1 tbsp salt
500ml (18fl oz) white wine vinegar

1 - Cut the vegetables into equal-sized pieces, about 4 x 1cm (1½ x ½in). Put in a large salad bowl. Sprinkle with the salt and vinegar and turn, mixing so that the salt is dissolved and the vegetables are evenly coated in the dressing.

2 - Leave to marinate for a minimum of 2 hours before serving.

GRANDE DISTILLERIE
DE LA SOURRA

BOUKHA
L'OASIS
BOKOBSA
PRODUCTION

EAU DE VIE DE FIGUE
100cl.   36%vol.

Kefta de poisson   Fish balls

Fish balls are one of the most loved traditional starters in Jewish cooking. It is important that the oil is hot enough to crisp the coating immediately, otherwise it seeps inside, with greasy results. When perfect, you get a delicious fishy mouthful, slightly crunchy on the outside and meltingly soft within.

serves 8 (about 40 fish balls)

500g (1lb 2oz) whiting fillets, roughly chopped

2 large onions, peeled and finely chopped

leaves from a small bunch of flat leaf parsley, finely chopped

2–3 slices stale bread, soaked in water, then patted dry and broken up

2 eggs, beaten

1 tsp harissa (see page 186)

½ tsp ground cinnamon

1 tsp turmeric

small handful dried rose petals (optional)

salt and ground black pepper, to taste

handful of breadcrumbs (optional)

vegetable oil, for deep frying

lemon wedges, to garnish

1 - Place the fish, onion, parsley and soaked bread pieces in a bowl, mix and knead together.

2 - Add the eggs, harissa, spices, rose petals (if using), salt and pepper. If the mixture becomes too sloppy, add some dry breadcrumbs.

3 - Make little balls from the mixture, about 3cm (1¼in) in diameter, rolling them between the wet palms of your hands.

4 - Pour sufficient vegetable oil to half-fill a deep frying pan. Heat the oil over a medium–high heat and lower the fishballs carefully into the oil. Deep-fry the balls for 5 minutes, or until they are crisp and brown, turning them occasionally, then remove with a slotted spoon, drain and lay on paper towels to absorb any excess oil. Serve hot, garnished with lemon wedges.

Banatages   Potato croquettes

These tempting croquettes have just a hint of North Africa in them thanks to the turmeric, although this can be replaced with garlic for more punch. Frying is typical of Jewish-Tunisian cuisine, but you can offset the oiliness by serving the croquettes with a fresh green salad.

serves 5–6 (about 16 croquettes)

vegetable oil, for deep frying
100g (3½oz) minced beef
2 tbsp finely chopped flat leaf parsley leaves
1 large onion, peeled and finely chopped
salt and ground black pepper, to taste
600g (1lb 5oz) potatoes, peeled and boiled
1 tsp turmeric
lemon juice, to taste
2 eggs, beaten
2 eggs, hard boiled, cut into eighths
5–6 tbsp breadcrumbs, for coating

1 - Heat a little vegetable oil in a frying pan. Lightly fry the minced beef over a medium heat, along with the parsley, onion, salt and pepper, then cover with water. Simmer hard until the water has evaporated. Remove from the heat and set aside.

2 - Mash the potatoes, season with salt, pepper, turmeric and lemon juice, and stir in half the beaten egg. Mix well.

3 - Form flat little 'biscuits' of the potato mixture about 6cm (2½in) in diameter and add in the centre about ½ tbsp of the meat stuffing and a piece of hard-boiled egg, then roll up completely into a small sausage shape, making sure no stuffing is visible. Dip each croquette in the remaining beaten egg and then in the breadcrumbs to coat.

4 - Pour sufficient vegetable oil to half-fill a large saucepan. Heat the oil and deep-fry the croquettes over a medium–high heat, turning frequently, until golden. Remove the croquettes with a slotted spoon, drain and place on paper towels to absorb the excess oil.

5 - Serve warm with an extra squeeze of lemon juice.

Tajine kares   Lemon chicken

This is a quiet, surprisingly delicate dish compared with North Africa's usual racy flights of flavours. The chicken can be replaced with cubed lamb, and in either case should be served with steamed couscous (see page 186) flavoured with finely chopped fresh mint or rose water.

serves 4

3–4 tbsp olive oil, plus extra for frying
1 tsp *tabel* (see page 187)
½ tbsp turmeric
2 garlic cloves, peeled and finely chopped
salt and ground black pepper, to taste
6 chicken breasts
2 large onions, peeled and finely chopped
4 tsp caster sugar
½ pumpkin, peeled, deseeded and diced
1 large unwaxed lemon, quartered
handful of flat leaf parsley leaves, chopped, to garnish

1 - Mix the olive oil with the *tabel*, turmeric, garlic, salt and pepper. Marinate the chicken breasts in this mixture for about 30 minutes.

2 - Meanwhile, in a large saucepan, lightly fry the onion in a little olive oil, sprinkle with a little salt and, when turning golden, add the sugar. Stir until it dissolves. Add the pumpkin and lemon quarters, stirring continuously for a few minutes.

3 - Cover the mixture with water and simmer hard for 10–15 minutes to reduce the liquid. Remove from the heat, stir in 1–2 tbsp cold water and transfer to a blender. Whiz for about 1 minute to obtain a thick cream.

4 - Cut the chicken breasts into 2½cm (1in) chunks. Heat a little olive oil in a frying pan and fry the chicken pieces over a low heat, turning occasionally. After about 20 minutes, or until cooked through, transfer to a saucepan and add the warm cream. Adjust the seasoning, adding more salt or sugar if necessary, and garnish with the chopped parsley. Serve immediately.

Mechmachia   Lamb with pumpkin and apricots

This dish combines meat with sweet dried fruits, while caramelized onion adds a melt-in-the-mouth quality. It is best eaten with steaming couscous (see page 186) scattered with fried almonds.

serves 4

vegetable oil, for frying
2 large onions, peeled and finely chopped
salt, to taste
4 tsp caster sugar
250g (9oz) pumpkin, peeled, deseeded and grated
500g (1lb 2oz) boned shoulder of lamb, cut into small chunks
50g (1¾oz) raisins
1 litre (1¾ pints) water
100g (3½oz) pitted prunes, soaked in water
100g (3½oz) dried, pitted apricots, soaked in water

1 - Heat the vegetable oil in a large casserole dish. Lightly fry the onion, sprinkled with a little salt, until golden. Add the sugar and stir to caramelize the mixture.

2 - Add the pumpkin, stirring well over a medium heat to bind the mixture.

3 - Add the lamb, cook for 5 minutes, then add the raisins and water. Reduce the heat and simmer for 45 minutes. When the lamb is cooked, add the prunes and apricots and cook for 2 more minutes.

Ganaouia   Beef and okra stew

If you cannot find small okra, then chop larger ones in half.

serves 6

5 tomatoes
2 tbsp vegetable oil
5 large onions, peeled and chopped
1kg (2lb 4oz) stewing beef, cut into large chunks
10 garlic cloves, peeled and coarsely chopped
1 tsp salt
600g (1lb 5oz) small okra, topped and tailed

1 - Make a cross at the base of each tomato and plunge them into boiling water for 30 seconds. Transfer to cold water. Drain and remove the loosened skins. Chop roughly.

2 - Heat the vegetable oil in a casserole dish and fry the onion over a low heat until soft. Add the beef, cook for 1–2 minutes, stirring continuously, then add the tomatoes and garlic. Cook for a further 5 minutes, add salt, then sufficient water to cover. Simmer over a low heat for 1 hour.

3 - Add the okra and simmer gently for a further 20–30 minutes.

Crêpes à la confiture d'oranges
Orange crêpes

These little pancakes spiked with orange peel demand to be eaten and eaten – make them in large batches! Place a dollop of marmalade (or other jam) in the centre of each one and roll it up with your fingers. Make them about 15cm (6in) in diameter. Jacob serves his with jam made from bergamots, a slightly sour citrus fruit with aromatic peel that produces the bergamot oil used in Earl Grey tea.

serves about 6 (about 20 crêpes)

200g (7oz) plain flour
½ packet easy-blend yeast
½ tsp ground cinnamon
½ tsp ground aniseed
grated zest of 1 unwaxed orange
½ tsp ground rose petals (optional)
3 eggs, beaten
2 tbsp honey
1 tbsp crème fraîche or soya cream
about 500ml (18fl oz) water
butter, for cooking
marmalade (see opposite) or jam, to serve

1 - Sift the flour into a large bowl and mix with the yeast, cinnamon, aniseed, orange zest and ground rose petals (if using). Mix the beaten eggs with the honey and crème fraîche or soya cream. Make a well in the centre of the dry ingredients, add the egg mixture and pour in most of the water. Gradually whisk the dry ingredients into the liquid to form a fluid batter, adding more water if necessary. Leave to stand for 30 minutes.

2 - Preheat the oven to 110°C/225°F/Gas mark ¼. In a small frying pan, heat a little butter over a medium heat. Use a small espresso coffee cup (about 5 tbsp in capacity) to measure out the batter for each crêpe. Pour one quantity of measured batter into the frying pan and cook for 1–2 minutes, then flip the crêpe and cook for another minute. Transfer the cooked crêpe to a plate and keep warm in the oven while preparing the rest. Add more butter to the frying pan when necessary.

3 - Serve the crêpes on a large plate with marmalade or jam.

Confiture d'oranges   Seville orange marmalade

makes 2kg

2kg (4lb 8oz) Seville oranges, halved
2 lemons, halved
3 tsp whisky
600g (1lb 5oz) granulated sugar

1 - Squeeze the oranges and lemons to obtain their juice, setting aside the pips and peel. Add the whisky and sugar to the juice, then cover and chill in the refrigerator for 24 hours.

2 - Tie the pips in muslin and suspend from the handle of a saucepan so the parcel is inside. Add the juice and simmer for 1 hour. Meanwhile, very finely chop the orange and lemon peel.

3 - Add the chopped peel to the pan and simmer for a further 30 minutes.

4 - Put the marmalade into sterilized jars and seal to make airtight.

TRIPOLI

طرابلس

Fozia Shwek

'MEN ONLY HELP IN THE KITCHEN WHEN THEY'RE HUNGRY!'

There is a romantic background to Fozia Shwek's culinary skills. After she first met and married Fouad 17 years ago, they spent months zigzagging across the Mediterranean. They only stopped their voyaging when Fozia's first pregnancy was well advanced. A personal fortune? Oil wealth? Far from it. Fouad's job as a radio officer on cargo and passenger ships meant they travelled together from Libya to Italy, Spain, Malta, Greece, Turkey and Portugal. As a result, the impressionable Fozia gained a strong taste for foreign cultures and cuisines – a rarity for a young woman in 1980s' Tripoli.

Widening her beautiful eyes and with a big smile, 40-year-old Fozia recalls that period. 'It was a wonderful life,' she muses. 'I liked Italy most because of the restaurants and general lifestyle. They eat and dress really well, and of course a lot of their food is familiar to us. And in close second place came Spain.' Fouad, 50, is even more at home with foreign cultures, having spent 10 years studying and working in northern England. Over 25 years later, his English accent unusually mixes Lancashire with Tripoli and he confesses to having acquired a taste for sirloin steak for breakfast from a cosseting landlady. 'And the Blackpool illuminations – have you seen them?' he exclaims, his eyes lighting up. 'And Ken Dodd?' He laughs, knowing that things have moved on in England as much as in Libya.

Today their life might be more sedentary but it is no less energetic: Fouad's latest venture is co-managing a new Libyan restaurant, where he keeps an eagle eye on the kitchen. Situated in an attractive square of the old medina, just behind the massive hulk of the fort, the restaurant is only about 10 minutes' drive from the modern quarter, where their family flat is located. In contrast to the restaurant fare, what they eat at home is not always traditionally Libyan. It has become all too easy to pick up imported foods from one of Tripoli's huge El Mansari supermarkets, a modern, well-stocked affair that even sells camel meat. But for fresh fruit and vegetables, Fozia and Fouad remain faithful to a roadside market a short drive away. Here, immaculate produce neatly packed in small wooden crates is sold from the backs of pick-up trucks and car boots as well as from a few stalls. The highway location makes it a kind of drive-in farmers' market, typical of oil-rich Libya's car-dependent lifestyle, with squeals of brakes when one of North Africa's worst drivers spots his favourite apricots on sale.

Drawing the line between the couple's respective culinary exploits is almost impossible as Fouad taught Fozia virtually all the recipes she knows. However, true to traditional Islamic society, Fozia is the one who wields the pots and pans most of the time. Being a university graduate, she could easily work as a teacher, but for the moment she spends her days homebound looking after their four children, aged between 5 and 16. 'No more!' she smiles. 'As we both come from huge families of 11 and 9 children, we feel four's plenty.'

The big exception to her domestic routine comes on Friday, the Muslim sabbath, when Fouad has a day off from the restaurant and they make family outings in their beaten-up Toyota. In summer (starting in late May) the destination is often the beach, where Fozia and the children all go swimming. Spring and autumn see them picnicking in leafy corners of the outlying countryside; grilled chicken, mixed salad and *imbakbka* (macaroni cooked in a meat or fish sauce) make up the simple hamper. A more sociable alternative, at any time of year, is making lunch and eating at the large new house of Fouad's business partner, Sadak, on the rural outskirts of Tripoli.

Sadak's poised, friendly wife Namat, a gynaecologist at Tripoli's main hospital, pitches in with Fozia to prepare a bountiful meal for both their broods while Raslam, a calm young Moroccan house-help, controls the washing up. A trail of children come and go, curious to see what is being prepared but more interested in the pool outside. There is no formality and the pace is unhurried, light-hearted, seemingly chaotic: typically Libyan, in fact. As the women chat and chop in the kitchen, the men talk business and joke out in the garden; despite education and emancipation, old habits die hard. Then, when the *muezzin* kicks in, Fouad and Sadak disappear to the mosque for midday prayers. On their return, the couscous is well advanced so, determined to contribute, Fouad pounces upon it to break up the grain, add more rose water and vegetable juice, and then return it to steam.

'Men only help when they're hungry,' comments Fozia, drily, then turns to peel a couple of bananas and hand them to two increasingly ravenous boys. Adjusting her headscarf, which comes on and off depending on who is around, and which she admits to disliking, she goes back to stuffing green peppers. 'This is the first thing I learned to make and I still really enjoy it, along with lasagne and *imbakbka*,' she says with a smile. 'We eat masses of different pastas in Libya – it's a hangover from the Italian days. The European desserts I enjoy making are cheesecake and trifle. Libyan desserts are often fresh fruit or bought pastries but *basbousa* (semolina and honey cake – see page 185) is the big exception, which I make often – it's easy and the children love it.'

Eventually, the numerous courses all come together on time. With no lingering over glasses of wine, lunch is dispatched in fast and furious fashion, with little ceremony. Spoons are laid out but fingers are the rule and there are no individual plates. The mountainous couscous, the centre of the meal, is heaped up in a wide ceramic bowl. 'We all eat out of the same dish – communal activities are actually an important part of Islam,' points out Fouad. 'Eating together is essential as it is about sharing.' With the copious lunch consumed down to the last grain of couscous and the dishes stacked in the kitchen, Fozia and Namat retire to a cool Arab-style room where they stretch out on long red velour sofas, gossip, giggle and eventually sink into well-deserved siestas.

Fozia's fridays represent a halfway world built on a strict Muslim base but with countless flashes of Western society. What both facets share is the simple yet gloriously fresh food in quantities fit for a pasha. Despite this, she hints at the tedium of daily cooking and how she longs for a different life. Her travels clearly left their mark, giving the normally cheerful, outspoken Fozia the odd moment or two of wistfulness.

TRIPOLI

Gaddafi's the boss here, no doubt about it. His image shadows you from airport to hotel lobby, from cyber café to medina shop. Swathed in Tuareg turban and robe (along with his signature sunglasses – Ray Ban or wraparound), he is clearly proud of his tribal origins. So it is not surprising to hear it said that he enjoys simple food – and whatever he eats will be washed down with mint tea, as alcohol is forbidden by his *Green Book*.

Not all Libyans follow their leader's example, as homemade hooch (similar to Irish *potcheen*) is far from unknown. However, the big public indulgence, other than hookah pipes, is seafood. Three quarters of Libya's five million people live along the 2,000km coastal belt, the longest coastline of the Mediterranean. Fresh fish is both a passion and an industry, as witnessed at daybreak when trawlers unload their overnight catch at the old harbour of Tripoli. Buyers from Tunisia and as far away as Japan snap up gargantuan tuna fish, lethal-looking swordfish, sea bass, amberjack, red and grey mullet, skate, squid, monkfish and lobster. The variety, quality and quantity are spectacular.

The teeming fish market takes place in the shadow of an ancient fort that is a synopsis of the tumultuous history of Tripolitania, the region surrounding the capital. Founded by the Romans, the fort was rebuilt by the Catholic Knights of St John, occupied for 300 years by the Ottomans, renovated by the Italians and now, under the Great Socialist Jamahiriya ('state of the masses') of Colonel Gaddafi, has been transformed into a museum. A star exhibit, alongside the graceful Roman statues, is the rusty VW Beetle in which Gaddafi led the 1969 revolution. Behind the fort unfolds the medina, a typical North African maze that extends north-west past hookah cafés and a vast jewellery souk to the Roman arch of Marcus Aurelius and the Gurgi mosque, a glittering Ottoman relic. The heart of the medina, where blind alleyways proliferate, is the domain of sub-Saharan Africans, a reflection of Gaddafi's political focus, now directed towards the rest of the African continent rather than Libya's Arab cousins.

Sweeping majestically around a wide bay, the site of Tripoli mesmerized first the Phoenicians, around 500 BC, then the Romans. Apart from irrigating massive olive plantations (today Libya has some eight million trees), the Romans built elaborate and spectacular towns at Leptis Magna and Sabratha, respectively east and west of today's capital and at the top of the Mediterranean's Roman ruins league table. En route to Leptis stands Gaddafi's old compound, bombed in 1986 by the Americans, while his new fortress, bristling with watchtowers, lies to the west. Between the two extremities, four-lane highways curl like ribbons along the seafront and pander to the great Libyan love of driving. Petrol is cheap and, as not much else goes on, an evening's entertainment might be a couple of hours' cruising to the stereo sounds of Yusuf Islam (aka Cat Stevens), Madonna or the Egyptian diva Oum Kalthoum. The evening ends in a squeal of brakes outside an air-conditioned pastry shop: Libya's gastronomic trump card. The Tunisians may look down on their neighbours, but Tripoli has the best patisseries and *loukoum* (Turkish delight) in the Maghreb. Who knows, maybe even the Colonel occasionally indulges.

الملازم معمر القذافي يقوم بتوزيع المناشير بسيارته في م

Shorba hoüt   Fish soup

The stunning array of seafood at Tripoli's harbourside fish market puts fish soup at the top of the menu in the Libyan capital. This version uses an array of spices to enhance the flavour of the fish, with cumin dominating.

serves 4

> **1 onion, peeled and finely chopped**
> **olive oil, for frying**
> **1 tsp ground coriander**
> **1 tsp turmeric**
> **1 tsp chilli powder or paprika**
> **1 tsp ground cumin (see page 186)**
> **1 tbsp tomato purée**
> **2 garlic cloves, peeled and crushed**
> **1 litre (1¾ pints) water**
> **500g (1lb 2oz) flaky white fish, such as sea bream, scaled, gutted, cleaned and cut into chunks**
> **1 fish head (retained from the prepared fish)**
> **4 large shelled prawns, uncooked`**
> **juice of ½ lemon**

1 - In a deep saucepan, fry the onion in a little olive oil over a medium heat for a few minutes, until soft, then add the spices, tomato purée and garlic. Stir together then add the water, fish, fish head and prawns.

2 - Simmer over a low heat for about 45 minutes. Remove the prawns and set aside. Discard the fish head, bones and skin before pouring the rest of soup through a fine sieve, being careful to remove any stray tiny bones.

3 - Put a prawn and a drizzle of lemon juice into each bowl before serving.

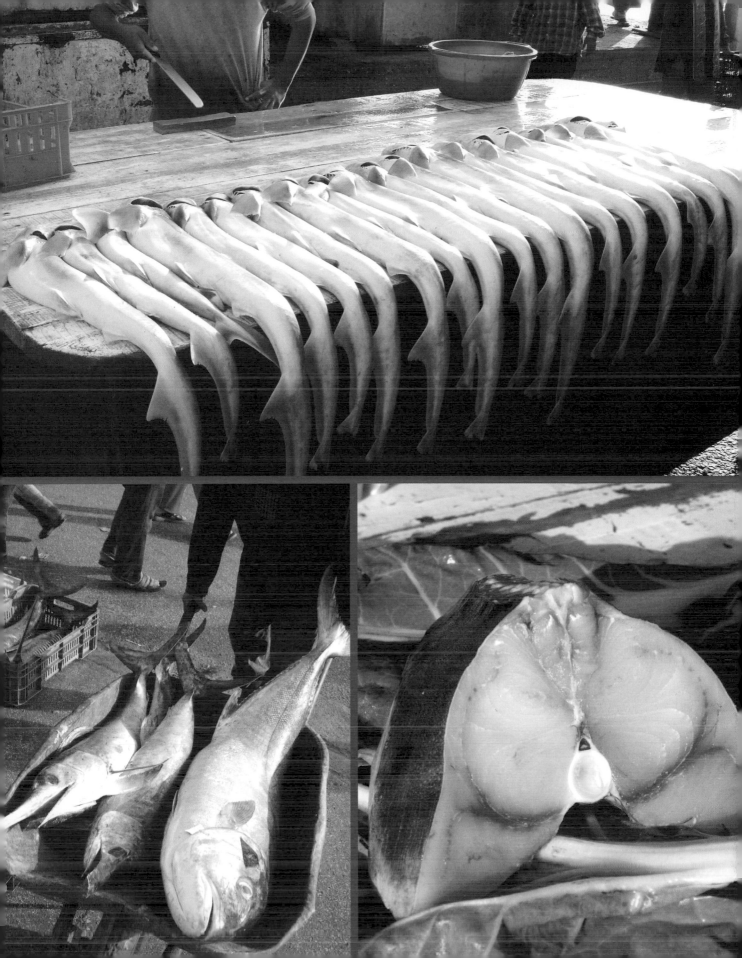

Shorba Libiya   Libyan soup

If you ever travel extensively in Libya, this soup will soon become familiar as it appears, in different versions, at the start of virtually every meal. Nourishing, flavoursome and easy to make, it is a classic Bedouin brew. Try to use dried mint, which adds a zingier and more exotic flavour than parsley.

serves 4–6

3 tbsp olive oil

1 large onion, peeled and finely chopped

500g (1lb 2oz) stewing lamb, finely chopped

1 x 200g (7oz) can chickpeas, drained and rinsed

2–3 tbsp tomato purée

1 tsp ground coriander

1 tsp turmeric

½ tsp chilli powder

salt, to taste

about 1 litre (1¾ pints) water

1 tbsp dried mint, or a handful of chopped flat leaf parsley leaves

squeeze of lemon juice (optional)

1 - Heat the oil in a frying pan over a medium heat and fry the onion for a few minutes, until soft. Add the lamb, chickpeas, tomato purée, spices and salt, and cook for a few minutes more, stirring occasionally.

2 - Cover the mixture with water and simmer over a medium heat for 30–45 minutes, or until the lamb is cooked. Add extra water, if required. Adjust the seasoning, if necessary.

3 - When the dish is ready, stir in the dried mint or parsley, add a squeeze of lemon juice, if desired, and serve.

Zaaluk badinjan   Aubergine caviar

Aubergine was the most common vegetable in medieval Islamic cookbooks, from Baghdad to Andalucia, and its popularity survives in Arabian cooking today. For authenticity, eat this creamy dip as a shared, central dish, scooped up with hot, crisp flatbread. For a milder flavour, a more liquid texture and an Ottoman twist, stir in some plain yogurt before chilling.

serves 6

2–3 large aubergines, about 500g (1lb 2oz)
2–3 garlic cloves, peeled
pinch of salt
3 slices of white bread, without crusts, broken into breadcrumbs
3 tbsp lemon juice
5 tbsp extra-virgin olive oil
1 onion, peeled and finely chopped
3 tbsp chopped flat leaf parsley leaves
salt and ground black pepper, to taste
handful of pitted black and green olives, to garnish

1 - Preheat the oven to 180°C/350°F/Gas mark 4. Prick the aubergines with a fork a couple of times, then bake until soft (this takes about 45 minutes). Remove from the oven and cool slightly. Cut off the stalks, remove the skins and chop the flesh coarsely.

2 - Using a pestle and mortar, crush the garlic with a pinch of salt.

3 - In a large bowl, mix together the chopped aubergine and breadcrumbs. Add the lemon juice and olive oil, mixing well to coat the aubergine, then mash well with a fork, or whiz in a blender for a smoother consistency. Add the garlic and the remaining ingredients, apart from the olives. Mix well, cover and chill in the refrigerator.

4 - When chilled, taste the mixture and adjust the seasoning, if necessary. Garnish with the olives.

Mashi dolma   Stuffed courgettes and peppers

This classic Turkish dish was brought by the Ottomans but has undergone a Libyan makeover.
The steamed version is deliciously moist and the mint makes it refreshing on a hot summer's day.
It is quite labour-intensive, so allow plenty of time for preparation.

serves 6

500g (1lb 2oz) green peppers
500g (1lb 2oz) small courgettes, trimmed
3 onions, peeled and finely chopped
leaves from a bunch of flat leaf parsley
500g (1lb 2oz) beef or lamb, minced
2 tbsp dried mint
150g (5½oz) cooked rice
1 tsp ground black pepper
pinch of salt
1 tsp chilli powder
2–3 large cabbage leaves
2 tbsp tomato purée
750ml–1 litre (1⅓–1¾ pints) water

1 - Prepare the peppers by cutting off the stalk and upper quarter, or 'lid', of each. Remove all the
    inner pulp and seeds, then rinse. Cut the courgettes across the middle (not lengthways) to
    obtain two round halves from each one and scoop out the cores.

2 - Blend the onion and parsley in a food processor, then mix with the minced meat, mint, cooked
    rice, black pepper and salt in large bowl. Use your hands to do this, ensuring that the minced
    meat is evenly dispersed.

3 - Fill the peppers and courgettes with the mixture, ensuring that it is compact.

4 - Place the cabbage leaves in the base of a wide, deep pan and stand the stuffed vegetables on
    top, positioning them upright and packing them close together. Dilute the tomato purée in the
    water and pour over the stuffed peppers and courgettes, filling the pan with water to reach
    about halfway up the vegetables.

5 - Cover the pan, bring the water to the boil, then simmer, for about 45 minutes. Preheat the oven
    to 190°C/375°F/Gas mark 5, 10 minutes before the end of the cooking time. At the end of the
    cooking time, transfer the vegetables to the oven to brown for about 10 minutes.

Gamberi limoun touma salsa   Garlic and lemon prawns

This is a wonderfully simple but utterly delicious way to cook prawns. What is essential for any kind of seafood is total freshness, which is easy in Libya with its 2,000km of coastline. You could also use cooked prawns, and grill or bake them for a shorter time. Fozia uses this as a starter, but it could make a good light lunch served with a green salad.

serves 4

> **juice of 1 lemon**
> **5–6 tbsp extra-virgin olive oil**
> **6–7 garlic cloves, peeled and coarsely chopped**
> **ground black pepper, to taste**
> **500g (1lb 2oz) tiger prawns, shells left on, uncooked**

1 - Mix the lemon juice, olive oil, garlic and pepper in a small bowl, then pour over the prawns.

2 - Leave the prawns to marinate overnight in the refrigerator.

3 - Grill the prawns for 3–4 minutes or bake for 5 minutes in the oven (preheated to 200°C/400°F/ Gas mark 6) in an oiled ovenproof dish. Serve warm.

Haraimi   Fiery fish

Haraimi means 'hot', or 'to make hot with chillies', so this recipe is more about the sauce than the fish.

serves 6

cloves from 1 small head of garlic, peeled
   and crushed
½ tbsp ground cumin (see page 186)
salt, to taste
juice of 1 lemon
1kg (2lb 4oz) whole snapper, grey mullet,
   or grouper, scaled, gutted and cleaned
2 tbsp olive oil

1 onion, peeled and finely chopped
2 tbsp tomato purée
2 tomatoes, peeled with a vegetable
   peeler, deseeded and chopped
½–1 tsp chilli powder
½ tsp turmeric
1 tsp ground caraway seeds

1 - Mix half the crushed garlic with the cumin, salt and lemon juice. Rub this mixture into the fish and leave to marinate for 10–15 minutes.

2 - Heat the olive oil in a frying pan over a medium heat, add the onion and remaining garlic and fry until golden. Add all the other ingredients, except the fish, stirring continuously. Add about 600ml (20fl oz) just-boiled water and stir for 5–10 minutes until you have about 500ml (18fl oz) of sauce. Once the mixture has combined, reduce the heat, cover and simmer for 10 minutes.

3 - Lay the fish in the pan, cover and poach for 20–25 minutes, until cooked.

Fasoulia   Lamb and white bean stew

Simple and nourishing, this is a typical Libyan hybrid, halfway between a soup and a stew.

serves 4

1 onion, peeled and chopped
vegetable oil, for frying
600g (1lb 5oz) stewing lamb, cut into
   large chunks
2 tomatoes, chopped
1½ tbsp tomato purée
5 garlic cloves, peeled and crushed
¼ tsp chilli

1 tsp turmeric
2–3 cloves
500g (1lb 2oz) dried white beans,
   soaked overnight, drained and rinsed
salt and ground black pepper, to taste
flat leaf parsley leaves, chopped,
   to garnish

1 - Fry the onion in a little vegetable oil until soft. Add the lamb, tomatoes, tomato purée, garlic and spices and stir continuously for a few minutes over a medium heat.

2 - Add enough water to cover the ingredients generously, then add the beans, salt and pepper.

3 - Simmer the mixture, covered, for about 45 minutes, adding more water, if necessary. Check that the lamb and beans are cooked through, garnish with chopped parsley and serve warm.

Cuscusy lahem Lamb couscous

It's hard to circumvent the use of a couscoussier – a large steamer, which allows the couscous grain in the upper section to be flavoured by the steaming vegetables below. The alternative is to cook the vegetables in one pan and the couscous in another in a little water over a low heat, though this will never be as good. Fozia and Fouad's method needs constant attention: it's a good dish for two cooks. The result is a sumptuous Libyan (and North African) classic.

serves 8

2–3 tbsp vegetable oil

8–10 onions, peeled and sliced

750g (1lb 10oz) shoulder of lamb, cut into large pieces

220g (8oz) dried chickpeas, soaked overnight, drained and rinsed

5 heaped tbsp tomato purée

1 heaped tbsp chilli powder

1 tsp turmeric

salt, to taste

500ml (18fl oz) water

500g (1lb 2oz) couscous

250ml (9fl oz) warm water (previously boiled)

2 tbsp olive oil

1kg (2lb 4oz) mixed seasonal vegetables, such as pumpkin, courgettes, aubergines, carrots, turnips and potatoes, peeled and chopped into equal-sized chunks

2 tbsp salted butter

1 tsp ground cinnamon

2–4 tbsp rose water, or to taste

1 - Heat the vegetable oil in a large, deep saucepan and add the onion, lamb, chickpeas, tomato purée, chilli powder, turmeric and salt. Cook over a medium heat for 10–15 minutes, stirring occasionally. Add the water, cover and simmer for a further 15 minutes.

2 - Meanwhile, in a bowl, soak the couscous in the warm water for 10 minutes. Add the olive oil and rub the grain between your hands to break up any lumps. Set aside for 15–20 minutes.

3 - Stir the vegetables into the meat, adding extra water if necessary to cover all the ingredients.

4 - Spoon the couscous into a steamer above the lamb and vegetable mixture, and cook the whole lot for 15 minutes. Remove the couscous, return to the bowl, add the butter, cinnamon, rose water and 2 ladlefuls of the meat-cooking juices. Stir and return to the steamer. Cook the whole lot again for a further 10–15 minutes. Ensure the chickpeas and lamb are cooked.

5 - Transfer the couscous to a large, wide serving bowl. Turn it vigorously with a wooden spoon to break up any lumps, gradually spooning over the juice and chickpeas from the lamb and vegetable mixture. Adjust the salt and add more rose water, if necessary.

6 - Arrange the meat and vegetables over the couscous and pour over the remaining juice.

Basbousa   Semolina and honey cake

Countless variations of this recipe are found across the Middle East, from Turkey to Egypt and North Africa. There's a very good reason for this, as it is one of those simple cakes that everyone loves to devour. Try to use demerara sugar as it works particularly well. The syrup of honey and orange-blossom water is typical of the Maghreb, but can be substituted by a less fragrant, less sweet mixture of honey, water and lemon juice. You can also add finely grated lemon zest to the semolina mix, if desired.

serves 6–8 (12–16 pieces)

200g (7oz) semolina
100g (3½oz) demerara or caster sugar
100g (3½oz) plain flour
28g (1oz) ground almonds
1 tsp baking powder
50g (1¾oz) butter, melted
150ml (5fl oz) milk
50g (1¾oz) blanched almonds, to decorate
mint tea, to serve

syrup:
150g (5½oz) clear honey
100ml (3½fl oz) water
2 tbsp orange-blossom water

1 - Preheat the oven to 180°C/350°F/Gas mark 4. In a large bowl, mix the semolina, sugar, flour, ground almonds and baking powder. Stir in the melted butter. Gradually add the milk, stirring continuously to ensure there are no lumps, to give a stiff but malleable consistency.

2 - Spoon the mixture into a greased square baking tin, smoothing the surface to ensure an even depth. Bake in the centre of the preheated oven for 25–30 minutes, or until the surface is golden. By baking a little longer the cake will gain a crunchier texture.

3 - To make the syrup, combine the honey and water in a small pan, bring to the boil and simmer for a few minutes. Add the orange-blossom water and set aside.

4 - When the cake is cooked, decorate the surface with blanched almonds, spaced at intervals to allow it to be cut into small squares. Drench the cake in the syrup and return to the oven for a further 5 minutes. Leave to cool then cut into pieces. Serve with mint tea.

NORTH AFRICAN BASICS

ALMONDS, TOASTING

Cover the base of a frying pan with a thin film of vegetable oil, heat until it is just sizzling, then toss in the almonds. Fry them on both sides until toasted an amber colour – about 5 minutes. Remove with a slotted spoon and drain on paper towels before using. Alternatively you can heat them carefully for a few minutes in a hot oven or under the grill, taking care to ensure they do not burn.

COUSCOUS

Couscous (*kuskusu* or *seksu*) is the staple food for much of North Africa, although the cooking method (steaming over a pot of vegetables or meat) is also used throughout West Africa with other grains such as cracked barley or millet. Maghrebin couscous is made from coarsely ground durum wheat rolled into tiny pellets – what we know as semolina. If you want the lightest, fluffiest couscous (as it should be), it is hard to avoid the rather lengthy preparation process. It should ideally be cooked in three steaming stages as follows:

1. In a large wide bowl, rub water (about 200–250ml/7–9fl oz for 250g/9oz of couscous or just enough to moisten) and a tablespoon of olive oil into the grain, lifting and rubbing it repeatedly to distribute the moisture. Set aside to swell for 15 minutes or so.
2. Transfer to a double steamer, or couscoussier, with either water or vegetables simmering hard below. Steam for about 15 minutes leaving the lid off.
3. Return the couscous to the bowl, spread out with a wooden spoon, sprinkle with 3–4 tbsp more water, ½ tbsp olive oil and some salt. Lift and stir the grains, breaking up any lumps. Oil your hands to do this more effectively.
4. Return the couscous to the steamer to steam for another 15 minutes.
5. Put the couscous back in the bowl, add some liquid (water, vegetable juice or even rose water) to moisten thoroughly, break up any lumps with a wooden spoon and rework, separating the grains as much as possible.
6. Return to the steamer for a final 15-minute session.
7. Put in a large serving bowl (if possible wooden, to keep warm), lift the grains and turn over with a fork, adding some salted butter to make it really glisten.

CUMIN

Sometimes the cooks featured in this book buy cumin ready-ground and sometimes they toast and grind it themselves. To toast the seeds, put them in a dry, preheated frying pan for a few minutes. Transfer to a mortar and pound with a pestle until its terrific aroma is released and the seeds are fully crushed.

CURCUMA (TURMERIC)

Tunisians and Libyans use *curcuma* with alacrity while Moroccans don't use it at all. It is, in fact, turmeric, a major ingredient in curry. Recent research suggests that curcumin, a compound found in turmeric, may help reduce the brain damage associated with Alzheimer's disease, as well as having antioxidant properties that can help stave off other types of disease.

DRIED MINT

Dried mint is used in cooked dishes and occasionally in salads, above all in Tunisia. Hang bunches of fresh mint out to dry in the sun for a few days. You can crush them and use them immediately but, by pounding and crumbling the dried leaves then keeping them in an airtight container, the mint gains a much stronger flavour and fragrance.

HARISSA

Harissa is a fiery chilli paste that Tunisians love dolloping into their soups and stews. You can buy tinned harissa (a simple mix of chilli peppers, olive oil, garlic and salt) at the supermarket, but you can also make a superior version with a greater depth of flavour. The following recipe makes a good quantity to store away:

1 tbsp coriander seeds

1 tbsp caraway seeds

2 tsp cumin seeds

250g (9oz) fresh red chillies, roughly chopped

cloves from 1 head of garlic, peeled and roughly chopped

1 tbsp dried mint

½ bunch fresh coriander

1 tbsp salt

2–3 tbsp olive oil

Toast the seeds quickly in a saucepan without any oil for about 2 minutes until you can smell the aromas. Pound them into a powder using a pestle and mortar. Blend this with the remaining ingredients in a food processor, adding enough olive oil to make a stiff paste. Put in a sterilized jar, pouring a thin layer of olive oil over the surface to prevent it from drying out, then store in the refrigerator.

ORANGE BLOSSOM WATER

This scented water is made from the maceration and distillation of the fragrant flowers of the bitter (Seville) orange tree. It is widely used as a flavouring in patisserie and confectionery.

PRESERVED LEMONS

This indispensable element of Moroccan and Tunisian cooking is easy to make at home, although Western supermarkets now stock them. Use thin-skinned, untreated lemons, which should be thoroughly washed. With a sharp knife, incise two large crosses into the end of each lemon so that it is nearly cut into quarters but held together at the base. Sprinkle a good layer of salt into a large, sterilized preserving jar, pack the lemons tightly inside, adding more salt and filling with water (and optional coriander seeds, peppercorns and a bay leaf). Make sure the lemons are completely covered. Pour a layer of oil on top of the jar to help prevent mould forming. They will be ready to use in two weeks and last for up to a year. You can keep adding lemons to the pickle.

RAS-EL-HANOUT

The ingredients of this mixed spice (the name literally meaning 'roof of the shop') shift with the wind, the country and the humour of the cook. In Tunisia, a reduced version of pepper, cinnamon, cloves and dried rosebuds is used. In Morocco it achieves monumental proportions with anything between 15 and 30 ingredients, including cardamon, mace, nutmeg, pepper, *curcuma* (turmeric), ginger and belladonna berries. Other variations may include allspice, aniseed, belladonna leaves, black cumin seeds, black peppercorns, cantharides (a type of beetle), cayenne pepper, cinnamon, cloves, coriander seeds, earth almonds, galangal, ginger, dried lavender, mace, nutmeg, oris root and dried rose buds. Ras-el-hanout can be purchased by mail order or from one of the many food and spice markets in North Africa.

ROSE WATER

This scented water is made by the distillation of rose petals or by impregnation with oil of roses. It is widely used as a flavouring in patisserie and confectionery.

SAFFRON

This is Morocco's spice par excellence, hardly used elsewhere in North Africa. The fine red filaments from the stigma of a crocus are incredibly labour-intensive to produce and command very high prices. From Kashmir, where it originated, the *Crocus sativus* travelled through the Middle East to Moorish Spain, where it is still cultivated on a large scale, and then to Morocco. Production is in the Atlas Mountains and in Ourika, in the south.

SMEN

This clarified butter, used in Arabic and Maghrebi cookery, is made by simmering butter for about 15 minutes, skimming the oil off the top and straining it through muslin. It is salted just before setting, stirred with a wooden spoon and finally ladled into a container. The older the *smen*, the stronger and more rancid it tastes, therefore less is needed. Keeping it for years was once a sign of abundance and wealth, although few people make it themselves today.

TABEL

Tunisia's much loved 'four spices' mix is composed of 50 per cent coriander seeds, 25 per cent caraway seeds, 10 per cent dried red chillis (seeds removed) and 15 per cent peeled and dried garlic cloves. Mix, dry thoroughly in the sun, add some sea salt then whiz in a blender. Keep it in an airtight container.

RECOMMENDED RESTAURANTS

MARRAKECH

Dar Moha, 81 rue Dar El Bacha, Marrakech Medina, + (212) 2438 6400, www.darmoha.ma. The owner-chef, Mohammed Fedal, calls himself the 'little prince' of Morocco's nouvelle cuisine. Swiss-trained, he incorporates countless Western techniques and ideas without losing the local touch. A very upmarket riad that once belonged to Pierre Balmain, the French fashion designer.

El Fassia, 232 Ave Mohammed V, Guéliz, + (212) 4443 4060. This is a rare and welcome case of a restaurant where the food is just like home cooking. All the staff are women (it's a cooperative) and you can savour lamb confit, pigeon pastilla, one of ten tagines and a few couscous dishes too. Unlike its counterparts in the medina, this place is less about decor, more about what's on your plate.

Le Foundouk, 55 Souk Hal Fassi, Kat Bennahiid, Marrakech Medina, + (212) 2437 8190, www.foundouk.com. European but with a Moroccan soul, this beautiful old caravanserai mixes funky bar with an elegant candle-lit restaurant and, above, a panoramic roof-terrace where you can eat foie gras or pastilla – the range is vast.

L'Mimouna, 47 Place Qzadria, Place des Ferblantiers, Marrakech, + (212) 2438 6868. Silk divans, soft lights and low, hand-carved wooden tables are the setting for a sumptuous four-course menu which changes every couple of months. The background is an imposing palace with a terrace not to be missed. Perfect fluffy couscous and delicate flaky pastilla are the mainstays.

La Maison Arabe, 1 Derb Assehbe, Bab Doukkala, Marrakech Medina, + (212) 2438 7010, www.lamaisonarabe.com. One of the rarer breed of palace restaurants that concentrates on doing traditional cuisine to the highest possible standards. Formal and rather perfect.

Tobsil, 22 Derb Abdellah Ben Hassaien, Bab Ksour, Marrakech Medina, + (212) 4444 4052. Ochre walls, flunkies and no menu set the pace. This is regarded as one of Marrakech's top tables, even if the size of the set dinner can be too much, from mezze to pastilla, tagine, couscous and tea and pastries.

FEZ

Dar El Ghalia, 13/15 Ross Rhi, Medina de Fès, + (212) 3563 4167/3574 1574, www.maisondhotes.co.ma. One of the grand old traditional riads of Fez, with a fantastic rooftop restaurant overlooking the medina and the hills beyond. The hands of Khadouj and her boss, Monsieur Lebbar, are behind the excellent Fassi cuisine here.

La Maison Bleue, 2 Place de l'Istiqlal-Batha, Fez, + (212) 3563 6052, www.maisonbleue.com. The third of Fez's trio of top riad restaurants is in an overwhelmingly sumptuous setting. Ouds (traditional stringed instruments) are plucked in the background during dinner.

Riad Fès, 5 Derb Ben Slimane, Zerbtana, Fez, + (212) 3594 7610, www.riadfes.com. Delicate and beautifully presented, the dishes at this very palatial riad have a modern feel to them, although many of the recipes are 100 per cent traditional. Kenza may well be at the stoves.

Palais de Fès – Dar Tazi Hotel, 15 Makhfia Er'cif, Place Recif, Medina de Fès, + (212) 3576 1590. You can't beat the selection of delicious starter salads anywhere, and the views from the terraces and glassed-in restaurant are truly panoramic. Perfect for an evening which is sizzling hot, freezing cold or just raining.

TUNISIA

Au Bon Vieux Temps, 56 rue Hedi Zarrouk, Sidi Bou Said, + (216) 7174 4733. A romantic classic with fabulous views over the Bay of Tunis from the terrace. The cuisine verges on French–Tunisian fusion, with the accent on seafood, baked, spicy or with couscous.

Restaurant Dar Edhiaf, Place de la Colonne Romaine, Kheireddine Plage, La Goulette, + (216) 7127 6827, www.daredhiaf.com. Traditional restaurant in an old beachfront villa for sea bream stuffed with olives, mechouia, octopus salad, merguez tagine or stuffed leg of lamb. A Jacob Lellouche regular.

Dar El Jeld, 5–10, rue Dar el Jeld, Tunis El Medina, + (216) 7156 0916. Stunningly restored 18th-century riad on the edge of the medina. Tunisian specialities are cooked to perfection, ranging from a classic fluffy couscous to *kabkabou*, sea bass with tomato, capers and preserved lemon, or *marquit hloua*, a rich lamb stew. This is arguably the best and most elegant restaurant in and around Tunis, and a great favourite with Mina Ben-Miled.

Restaurant La Petite Etoile, La Goulette-Port + (216) 7173 6205. Smack on the harbour, an olive's throw from where the European ferries dock, this is another Jacob haunt. Seafood, of course, rules: *couscous au poisson*, baked fish from Sfax and squid; but carnivores despair not as *merguez* is also on the menu.

Restaurant Mohamed Salah El Abed, Souk Essakajine 2, Tunis El Medina. A cracking medina lunch place in a covered alley with kitchen opposite. Fantastic grilled lamb kebabs, Tunisian salad and cheerful waiters. Water or mint tea washes it down.

Restaurant M'Rabet, 26 rue Souk Etrouk, Tunis El Medina, + (216) 7156 1729. Beautiful colonnaded setting for mint tea and patisseries under chandeliers (and better than the mediocre upstairs restaurant).

LIBYA

Abia, Zanqa Souq, Tripoli Medina, + (218) 92 501 0736. Renowned little hole-in-the-wall restaurant serving sumptuous fish lunches and salads at knockdown prices.

Athar Restaurant, Marcus Aurelius Arch Square, Tripoli Medina, + (218) 91 444 7001. Upmarket restaurant at the top of the town, overlooking a stunning Roman triumphal arch. This is the rendezvous for Tripoli's movers and shakers.

Restaurant Essaa, Essaa Square, Tripoli Medina, + (218) 91 219 0683. Fouad and Sadak man the fort at this Libyan restaurant serving typical dishes in an attractive, traditional decor just behind the real fort. The café outside is a classic for hookah-puffing businessmen.

Restaurant Fès, Corinthia Bab Africa Hotel, Souk Al Thulatha, Al Gadim, Tripoli, + (218) 21 335 1990. Tripoli's only 5-star hotel, although you will be eating Moroccan, not Libyan fare, from pigeon pastilla to couscous and tagine.

Seafood Market Restaurants, Al Fatih highway, East Tripoli, + (218) 91 320 6971. Fresh-fish restaurants on the waterfront: you choose, they barbecue and serve. Great for an evening out of the centre.

INDEX

ACKNOWLEDGEMENTS

My thanks to supportive friends who gave advice and more, including Jules Wilson-Jones (there can be no calmer medina companion), Dominique Benedittini, Christoph Kicherer and Yves Marbrier for their generosity and serene Tunis home, and Yves Cardoso. Also to Kate and Alaa of Dar Seffarine for creating an unexpected second home in Fez and to Kenza Melehi and Abel Damoussi of Club Agafay for recognizing the vision from the start.

Above all my immense appreciation and gratitude go to all the cooks and, when apt, to their employers, for putting up with me, my questions and with Simon's lens. We were privileged to work beside them all – beaming Aicha, Latifa and her daughter-in-law Laila, Kenza and her employer Fouzia Sefrioui, Khadouj and her former employer Omar Lebbar, Dalila and her husband Ahmed, Mina and her charming assistant Sabiha, Jacob and his mother Lilie, and Fozia and her canny husband Fouad (who grasped the concept of the book so precisely). I miss all those fabulous meals.

I am also extremely grateful to Simon Wheeler for his equal measures of enthusiasm, energy, angst and wit, but above all for his fantastic pictures and fresh approach to design, to Nicky Collings for ever-perceptive comments and to Becca Spry for following the book through with her usual clarity of judgement and inimitable buoyancy.

Shukran!

Fiona Dunlop travels first and salivates second. She has written numerous travel guides and contributes to lifestyle books and magazines as well as to the travel pages of *The Sunday Telegraph*, *Financial Times* and *The Observer*. Following the success of *New Tapas*, an exploration of Spain's best tapas bars, *Medina Kitchen* is the result of a long fascination with North Africa, as well as dedicated evenings in the couscous dives of Paris during an extended 17-year stay. Between trips, Fiona now lives in London.